The Soft-Spoken
Parent

The Soft-Spoken Parent

More Than 50 Strategies to Turn Away Wrath

H. WALLACE GODDARD, PH.D.

Leatherwood Press books are available exclusively

through Deseret Book Distributors.

For details write or telephone

Deseret Book Distributors, 40 East South Temple

Salt Lake City, Utah 84111, (801) 534-1515

Leatherwood Press LLC

8160 South Highland Drive

Sandy, Utah 84093

www.leatherwoodpress.com

ISBN-10: 1-59992-001-8

ISBN-13: 978-159992-001-6

Designed by Andy Goddard

Printed in Malaysia

Acknowledgements

Thanks to the most patient and kind person I have ever known, my dear wife, Nancy. Thanks also to our children, their spouses, and their children for their patience with me as I learn to practice what I preach. Thanks to my wonderful parents and ancestors who planted a love of God deep in my soul. Thanks to those who have taught me about this important subject—Haim Ginott, Pahoran, Peter—and so many others. Most of all, thanks to the Lord Jesus Christ for his perfect example, teachings, and redemptive love.

A soft answer turneth away wrath:
but grievous words stir up anger.
Proverbs 15:1

Table of Contents

Introduction

We all get angry. Sometimes it is nothing more than simmering irritation. Other times it is fire in our soul. Our ears burn and every cell tenses.

Yet even as we ready for the holy battle, we have the sneaking suspicion that our anger is not good for us or for our unlucky target.

We are right. Anger is very destructive.

So this book is for normal parents—parents like me and you—who love their children but get angry too readily. This book is for parents like us who have gotten so upset about some minor offense that we have launched into an endless lecture quite heedless of the devastation we were heaping on our children. This is for parents who find themselves simmering with the combination of stress in their own lives and misdeeds in their children's lives.

This book is for parents like us who want their children to become good, caring, loving adults and wish that we were better parents so we didn't get in their way.

You're Not Alone

Haim Ginott, the parenting genius and author of several books, described our dilemma in the introduction to his classic *Between Parent and Child*: "No parent wakes up in the morning planning to make a child's life miserable. No mother or father says, 'Today, I'll yell, nag, and humiliate my child whenever possible.' On the contrary, in the morning many parents resolve, 'This is going to be a peaceful day. No yelling, no arguing, and no fighting.' Yet, in spite of good intentions, the unwanted war breaks out again. Once more we find ourselves saying things we do not mean, in a tone we do not like."[1]

In fact, those of us who are most vulnerable to anger may be those who have stronger emotions of all kinds. We love more passionately, we live more joyously. That is a blessing. But it must needs be that there is an opposite in all things. Along with the gift of fire (enthusiasm, passion, gusto, zeal), we have the challenge of channeling, managing, and training our fire.

Fire can warm and cook. It can also scorch and destroy. Let's begin by trying to better understand anger.

The Pleasure of Anger

There is something wonderfully satisfying about anger. Frederick Buechner said it elegantly: "Of the seven deadly sins, anger is possibly the most fun. To lick your wounds, to smack your lips over grievances long past, to roll over your tongue the prospect of bitter confrontations still to come, to savor to the last toothsome morsel both the pain you are given and the pain you are giving back—in many ways it is a feast fit for a king."[2]

The excesses of anger are captured in a story I read about a woman who returned damaged merchandise to a store. She launched into the customer service rep with a vengeance. He listened patiently. Finally, after several minutes of listening patiently, he interrupted her and asked, "Ma'am, suppose we refund your money, provide you another one without charge, close the store, and shoot the manager. Would that be satisfactory?"

Anger tends to take us over. It is much like throwing a match into dry tinder. It starts readily, grows quickly, and is hard to stop.

---

1   Ginott, Haim G., *Between Parent and Child* (New York: Three Rivers Press, 2003), xiii.
2   Frederick Buechner, *Wishful Thinking* (San Fransisco: Harper & Row, 1993), 2.

The Assumptions Behind Anger

Even as we violate our conscience by insulting those we love, it is quite possible for us to feel virtuous. We may think, "You are wrong or bad and I am helping you by straightening you out." Consider some of the common assumptions behind most anger.

1. Anger is real. Anger tends to feel wonderfully authentic. "This is truth. I hadn't seen it before. But now I do!" We discover that our child has stolen from a neighbor, hurt a sibling, or told a lie. We feel that flash of indignation. Suddenly it all makes sense. The child needs rebuke!

2. "I must be honest with you." When we discover something awful, it seems as if we must deal with it immediately. We need to talk about it. The "truth" explodes from us. We can't seem to keep it in.

3. "I must deal with anger by getting it out." "With all this feeling inside me, if I don't get it out, I'll explode." So I tell my child just what she has done wrong—in angry, indignant tones.

4. "After getting my anger out, I will feel better." Most of us assume that the expression of anger is cathartic. "After I have fully expressed my indignation, I will feel relieved and peaceful."

5. "After I've told you what's wrong with you, you can do better." It seems that our child has been blind to some truth that we have discovered. When we point out his error, he should be able to make better choices in the future.

Anger seemingly has all the satisfactions of a crusade: a worthy cause, plenty of emotion, an opportunity to make the world a better place, and a deep feeling of satisfaction.

Unfortunately for those of us who get angry readily, all of the five ideas above are almost entirely false. The crusade turns out to be a slaughter of innocents. The truths about anger are very different from the common beliefs.

The Truth about Anger

Years of research have helped us better understand anger. It is generally not the positive, beneficial force that many have believed it to be. The following propositions about anger are generally closer to the truth than those listed above.

1. Anger is a liar. Our thoughts when we are angry are not calm, sensible, or balanced. They are narrow and frequently irrational and unbalanced. "Rare is the person who can weigh the faults of others without putting his thumb on the scales," wrote Byron J. Langenfield.[3] We get taken hostage by an unhelpful emotion and our reason and civility break down. Instead of seeking understanding, we begin to seek a conviction of the person.

2. Angry times are bad times for honesty. Anger tends to focus on the negative. But the negative part is not the whole story. It is not even the most important part of the story. When we are angry is not the best time to say everything we are thinking.

3. There are ways to deal with anger besides pouring molten lava on those we love. The popular belief that if we do not express our anger, it will

---

3 http://www.quotationsbook.com/authors/4222/Byron_J._Langenfield/.

explode—or come out in sick forms—is simply mistaken. Anger is a little like tasting very hot soup. We must allow it to cool a little before we eat it or we will burn our mouths.

4. We often feel quite conflicted after we have blown up with people we love. After unloading on a child, our minds may be insisting that we were right and that they needed to hear it. But our hearts tell us that we have violated the contract of love. We have turned against those we swore to bless and protect, to encourage and to teach. Francis Bacon once said, "A man that studieth revenge keeps his own wounds green."[4]

5. When we get angry at our children, it often leaves them unmotivated, even despairing. Think about times you have been given an angry lecture. Were you energized and motivated by the tirade? Most likely you were hurt and your first thought was counter-anger or revenge. It is possible that you acquiesced, but you were probably not motivated or energized. The same is true with our children. When we unload on them, they don't usually feel encouraged. They probably feel burdened, hopeless, and angry.

As a wise man has said, being angry is like drinking poison and waiting for your enemy to die. Anger destroys us. It also damages our most cherished relationships. It gives control of our lives to irrational—and usually unrighteous—passion.

The Commandments about Anger

While the field of psychology has generally turned against anger rather recently, God has always been against it. The Savior taught, "Whosoever is angry with his brother without a cause shall be in danger of the judgment: and whosoever shall say to his brother, Raca, shall be in danger of the

---

4 "Francis Bacon Quotes," http://www.brainyquote.com/quotes/quotes/f/francisbac133639.html.

council: but whosoever shall say, Thou fool, shall be in danger of hell fire" (Matthew 5:22).

This is serious business. If we are angry with our brother we risk damnation. Some may cite the "without cause" clause in the scripture. But Jesus removed that clause when he came to the new world. (The clause also does not appear in many of the most ancient manuscripts of Matthew 5:22.)

The Book of Mormon records Jesus' words:

> Ye have heard that it hath been said by them of old time, and it is also written before you, that thou shalt not kill, and whosoever shall kill shall be in danger of the judgment of God;
>
> But I say unto you, that whosoever is angry with his brother shall be in danger of his judgment. And whosoever shall say to his brother, Raca, shall be in danger of the council; and whosoever shall say, Thou fool, shall be in danger of hell fire. (3 Nephi 12:21–22)

To translate the scripture into more modern parlance, one may say, "You may have thought that murder was the great sin but I tell you that anyone who is angry with his brother or sister is in danger of God's condemnation. If you call any brother empty or worthless, you risk facing condemnation. If you insult or judge another human, you put your own salvation in peril."

This is stern stuff. Society may excuse—even encourage and model—smart-alecky, diminishing, and sarcastic attacks on people. God condemns all of it.

God's view is made more clear by a challenging verse in the Book of Mormon: "Behold what the scripture says—man shall not smite, neither shall he judge; for judgment is mine, saith the Lord, and vengeance is mine also, and I will repay" (Mormon 8:20).

The Lord begins by establishing the scriptural basis of the command: "Behold what the scripture says." Then he tells us to stay out of the judging and punishing business. That should be left to him. Only One who knows everything and loves perfectly can be trusted with judgment and punishment.

But what about parenting? Isn't it necessary for us to judge and punish? I think the scriptural answer is "No." The more we parent in God's way the less we will need to judge and punish.

This may seem impossible. I hope you will read the 55 strategies in this book and consider God's divine method—inviting us to come out of the natural-man tendency to judge and condemn while inviting us into the light of loving and teaching.

The apostle Paul said it well: "And, ye fathers, provoke not your children to wrath: but bring them up in the nurture and admonition of the Lord" (Ephesians 6:4). Nurture and admonition! As you study the strategies described in this book, see if you can see nurture and admonition as the recurring themes. I believe that those two elements are essential in God's method of raising children.

To nurture a child suggests that we protect, support, and encourage that child. Nurture involves giving time, interest, and affection.

When the Lord speaks of admonition, I think he means to counsel, guide, advise, and caution our children. It is our job as parents to help our children be aware of dangers along the mortal journey. It is also our job to help our children be equipped with faith, hope, and love for the journey. We are our children's first and foremost teachers.

Neither nurture nor admonition justifies parental condemning. The Lord asks us to get out and stay out of the condemning business. His command is stern: "Wherefore, I say unto you, that ye ought to forgive one another; for he that forgiveth not his brother his trespasses standeth condemned before the Lord; for there remaineth in him the greater sin. I, the Lord, will forgive whom I will forgive, but of you it is required to forgive all men" (D&C 64:9–10).

Lest this counsel to avoid anger seem unconventional and eccentric, let's consider the counsel of contemporary church leaders and prophets. The following seven pages have quotes—some fairly lengthy—from church leaders. Each has great insight and is worthy of study. You may also choose to just read the highlighted portions to get the key ideas.

Leaders' Counsel about Anger

Joseph Smith: "All the religious world is boasting of righteousness: It is the doctrine of the devil to retard the human mind, and hinder our progress, by filling us with self-righteousness. *The nearer we get to our Heavenly Father, the more we are disposed to look with compassion on perishing souls; we feel that we want to take them upon our shoulders, and cast their sins behind our backs....* If you would have God have mercy on you, have mercy on one another."[5]

Joseph Smith: "Nothing is so much calculated to lead people to forsake sin as to take them by the hand, and watch over them with tenderness. When persons manifest the least kindness and love to me, O what power it has over my mind, while the opposite course has a tendency to harrow up all the harsh feelings and depress the human mind."[6]

Brigham Young: "I will here say to parents, that *kind words and loving actions towards children, will subdue their uneducated natures a great deal better than the rod, or, in other words, than physical punishment....* Children who have lived in the sunbeams of parental kindness and affection, when made aware of a parent's displeasure, and receive a kind reproof from parental lips, are more thoroughly chastened, than by any physical punishment that could be applied to their persons. It is written, that the Lord 'shall smite the earth with the rod of his mouth'.... *Kind looks, kind actions, kind words, and a lovely, holy deportment towards them, will bind our children to us with bands that cannot easily be broken;* while abuse and unkindness will drive them from us, and break asunder every holy tie, that should bind them to us, and to the everlasting covenant in which we are all embraced. If my family; and my brethren and sisters, will not be obedient to me on the basis of kindness, and a commendable life before all men,

---

5   *Teachings of the Prophet Joseph Smith*, ed. Joseph Fielding Smith (Salt Lake City: Deseret Book, 1976), 241, emphasis added.

6   *Teachings of the Prophet Joseph Smith*, ed. Joseph Fielding Smith (Salt Lake City: Deseret Book, 1976), 240.

and before the heavens, then farewell to all influence. Earthly kings and potentates obtain influence and power by terrorism, and maintain it by the same means. Had I to obtain power and influence in that way, I should never possess it in this world nor in the next."[7]

Brigham Young: "Mark the path in which a number of our boys have traveled, from the time they were eight or ten years of age, to sixteen, eighteen and twenty. Have they been caressed and kindly treated by their parents, sent to school, and when at home taught to read good books, taught to pray themselves, and to hear their parents pray? *Have they been accustomed to live and breathe in a peaceful, quiet, heavenly influence when at home?* No. Then can you wonder that your children are wild, reckless and ungovernable? They care not for a name, or standing in society. Every noble aspiration is blunted; for they are made to go here or there, like mere machines, at the beck and call of tyrant parents, and are uncultivated and uncivilized. This picture will apply to a few of our young men. *Let parents treat their children as they themselves would wish to be treated, and set an example before them that is worthy of you as Saints of God.* Parents are responsible before the Lord, for the way in which they educate and train their children, for "Lo, children are an heritage of the Lord; and the fruit of the womb is his reward. Happy is the man that hath his quiver full of them; they shall not be ashamed, but they shall speak with the enemies in the gate."[8]

Brigham Young: "Bring up your children in the love and fear of the Lord; *study their dispositions and their temperaments,* and deal with them accordingly, never allowing yourself to correct them in the heat of passion; *teach them to love you rather than to fear you,* and let it be your constant care that the children that God has so kindly given you are taught in their early youth the importance of the oracles of God, and the beauty of the

---

7 Brigham Young, *Journal of Discourses*, November 6, 1864, Vol.10, 360–361, emphasis added.
8 Brigham Young, *Journal of Discourses*, November 6, 1864, Vol.10, 361–362, emphasis added.

principles of our holy religion, that when they grow to the years of man and womanhood they may always cherish a tender regard for them and never forsake the truth. I do not wish you to lay the stress and importance upon outward ceremonies that many do. Parents, teach your children by precept and example, the importance of addressing the Throne of grace; teach them how to live, how to draw from the elements the necessaries of life, and teach them the laws of life that they may know how to preserve themselves in health and be able to minister to others. And when instructing them in the principles of the Gospel, teach them that they are true, truth sent down from heaven for our salvation, and that the Gospel incorporates every truth whether in heaven, in earth, or in hell; and teach them, too, that we hold the keys of eternal life, and that they must obey and observe the ordinances and laws pertaining to this holy Priesthood, which God has revealed and restored for the exaltation of the children of men."[9]

Brigham Young: "Parents should never drive their children, but lead them along, giving them knowledge as their minds are prepared to receive it. *Chastening may be necessary betimes, but parents should govern their children by faith rather than by the rod, leading them kindly by good example into all truth and holiness.*"[10]

Brigham Young: "In our daily pursuits in life, of whatever nature and kind, Latter-day Saints, and especially those who hold important positions in the Kingdom of God, should *maintain a uniform and even temper, both when at home and when abroad.* They should not suffer reverses and unpleasant circumstances to sour their natures and render them fretful and unsocial at home, speaking words full of bitterness and biting acrimony to their wives and children, creating gloom and sorrow in their habitations, making themselves feared rather than loved by their families. *Anger should never be permitted to rise in our bosoms, and words suggested by angry feelings*

---

9 *Discourses of Brigham Young*, ed. John A. Widtsoe (Salt Lake City: Deseret Book, 1954), 207, emphasis added.
10 *Discourses of Brigham Young*, ed. John A. Widtsoe (Salt Lake City: Deseret Book, 1954), 208, emphasis added.

should never be permitted to pass our lips. 'A soft answer turneth away wrath, but grievous words stir up anger.' 'Wrath is cruel, and anger is outrageous;' but 'the discretion of a man deferreth his anger; and it is his glory to pass over a transgression.'"[11]

Joseph F. Smith: "Now, this is the thought that I desire to express: Fathers, if you wish your children to be taught in the principles of the gospel, if you wish them to love the truth and understand it, if you wish them to be obedient to and united with you, love them! and prove to them that you do love them by your every word or act to them. *For your own sake, for the love that should exist between you and your boys—however wayward they might be, or one or the other might be, when you speak or talk to them, do it not in anger, do it not harshly, in a condemning spirit. Speak to them kindly; get them down and weep with them if necessary and get them to shed tears with you if possible. Soften their hearts; get them to feel tenderly toward you.* Use no lash and no violence, but argue, or rather reason—approach them with reason, with persuasion and love unfeigned. With these means, if you cannot gain your boys and your girls, they will prove to be reprobate to you; and there will be no means left in the world by which you can win them to yourselves. But, get them to feel as you feel, have interest in the things in which you take interest, to love the gospel as you love it, to love one another as you love them; to love their parents as the parents love the children. You can't do it any other way. You can't do it by unkindness; you cannot do it by driving; our children are like we are; we couldn't be driven; we can't be driven now. We are like some other animals that we know of in the world. You can coax them; you can lead them, by holding out inducements to them, and by speaking kindly to them, but you can't drive them; they won't be driven. We won't be driven. Men are not in the habit of being driven; they are not made that way."[12]

---

11 *Discourses of Brigham Young*, ed. John A. Widtsoe (Salt Lake City: Deseret Book, 1954), 203–04, emphasis added.

12 *Gospel Doctrine: Selections from the Sermons and Writings of Joseph F. Smith*, ed. John A. Widtsoe (Salt Lake City: Deseret Book, 1939), 316, emphasis added.

Introduction

Joseph F. Smith: "We all have our weaknesses and failings. Sometimes the husband sees a failing in his wife, and he upbraids her with it. Sometimes the wife feels that her husband has not done just the right thing, and she upbraids him. What good does it do? Is not forgiveness better? Is not charity better? Is not love better? Isn't it better not to speak of faults, not to magnify weaknesses by iterating and reiterating them? Isn't that better? and will not the union that has been cemented between you and the birth of children and by the bond of the new and everlasting covenant, be more secure when you forget to mention weaknesses and faults one of another? Is it not better to drop them and say nothing about them—bury them and *speak only of the good that you know and feel, one for another, and thus bury each other's faults and not magnify them; isn't that better?*"[13]

David O. McKay: "*Never must there be expressed in a Latter-day Saint home an oath, a condemnatory term, an expression of anger or jealousy or hatred. Control it! Do not express it!*"[14]

Howard W. Hunter: "To fully understand this gift of agency and its inestimable worth, it is imperative that we understand that *God's chief way of acting is by persuasion and patience and long-suffering, not by coercion and stark confrontation. He acts by gentle solicitation and by sweet enticement.* He always acts with unfailing respect for the freedom and independence that we possess. He wants to help us and pleads for the chance to assist us, but he will not do so in violation of our agency. He loves us too much to do that, and doing so would run counter to his divine character."[15]

Gordon B. Hinckley: "Never forget that these little ones are the sons and daughters of God and that yours is a custodial relationship to them, that he

---

13 *Teachings of Presidents of the Church: Joseph F. Smith* (Salt Lake City: The Church of Jesus Christ of Latter-day Saints, 1998), 180–81, emphasis added.
14 *Teachings of Presidents of the Church: David O. McKay* (Salt Lake City: The Church of Jesus Christ of Latter-day Saints, 2003), 229, emphasis added.
15 Howard W. Hunter, "The Golden Thread of Choice," *Ensign*, November 1989, 18, emphasis added.

was a parent before you were parents and that he has not relinquished his parental rights or interest in these little ones. *Now, love them, take care of them. Fathers, control your tempers, now and in all the years to come. Mothers, control your voices, keep them down. Rear your children in love, in the nurture and admonition of the Lord. Take care of your little ones, welcome them into your homes and nurture and love them with all of your hearts*"[16]

Gordon B. Hinckley: "Age does something to a man. It seems to make him more aware of the need for kindness and goodness and forbearance. *He wishes and prays that men might live together in peace without war and contention, argument and conflict.* He grows increasingly aware of the meaning of the great Atonement of the Redeemer, of the depth of his sacrifice, and of gratitude to the Son of God, who gave his life that we might live.

"I wish today to speak of forgiveness. I think it may be the greatest virtue on earth, and certainly the most needed. There is so much of meanness and abuse, of intolerance and hatred. There is so great a need for repentance and forgiveness. It is the great principle emphasized in all of scripture, both ancient and modern.

"*May God help us to be a little kinder, showing forth greater forbearance, to be more forgiving, more willing to walk the second mile, to reach down and lift up those who may have sinned but have brought forth the fruits of repentance, to lay aside old grudges and nurture them no more.*"[17]

Thomas S. Monson: "At times *the need for mercy can be found close to home and in simple settings.* We have a four-year-old grandson named Jeffrey. One day his fifteen-year-old brother, Alan, had just completed,

---

16 Gordon B. Hinckley, Salt Lake University Third Stake conference, 3 November 1996; in *Church News*, 1 March 1997, 2, emphasis added.
17 Gordon B. Hinckley, "Forgiveness," *Ensign*, November 2005, 81–82, emphasis added.

on the family computer, a most difficult and rather ingenious design of an entire city. When Alan slipped out of the room for just a moment, little Jeffrey approached the computer and accidentally erased the program. Upon his return, Alan was furious when he observed what his brother had done. Sensing that his doom was at hand, Jeffrey raised his finger and, pointing it toward Alan, declared from his heart and soul, 'Remember, Alan, Jesus said "Don't hurt little boys."' Alan began to laugh; anger subsided; mercy prevailed."[18]

The Lord Jesus Christ: "There shall be no disputations among you.... For verily, verily I say unto you, he that hath the spirit of contention is not of me, but is of the devil, who is the father of contention, and he stirreth up the hearts of men to contend with anger, one with another. Behold, this is not my doctrine, to stir up the hearts of men with anger, one against another; but this is my doctrine, that such things should be done away" (3 Nephi 11:28–30).

Getting Free of the Father of Contention

Anger often seems irresistible. A child breaks a glass or hits a sibling and we erupt. Can such an automatic process be interrupted? Can volcanic anger be replaced with civil helpfulness? It seems that it would be easier to turn the mighty Mississippi upstream than to redirect the energy of wrath. We feel helpless in the face of our passion.

The problem of anger doesn't actually begin with the misbehavior that seems to cause it. It begins much sooner. Often we remain quite unaware of the background of irritation in our moods that sets the stage for anger. Sometimes our children get the residue of disappointment from work or loneliness in our souls.

---

18 Thomas S. Monson, "Mercy—The Divine Gift," *Ensign*, May 1995, 54, emphasis added.

There is another problem with anger. We may be quite unaware of the assumptions that we impose on those around us. We each have a script filled with notions about how people should act. When someone acts differently, we may become quite indignant.

When we act as if everyone should follow our rules, we set ourselves up for chronic frustration. There is a devious kind of pride in imposing our assumptions on everyone around us. In contrast, humility is a wonderful openness. We are more free to appreciate the diverse ways that people— including our children—think and act.

For example, a mother awoke on her birthday smelling the aromas of a delightful breakfast. She rested in bed anticipating a birthday surprise. After a long wait, one of the children came into her room, "As a birthday surprise, we cooked our own breakfast."

The mother could be quite angry that the children did not bring her any breakfast. Or she can be grateful for the children's growing thoughtfulness and self-sufficiency. Of course she might also tell them that she loves to have breakfast with them and would be glad to be included next time.

You can see the vital role of humility. When we are humble—when we don't insist on having the world operate by our rules—we are less likely to be irritated by differences. We are less likely to impose our meanings on someone else's behavior. The anger problem has deep roots—way down into our assumptions.

At the heart of much of our anger is a painfully human reaction. A child spills a glass of milk and, somewhere in our souls, we react: "How could you do this to me?" Of course we have been trained to use other words: "You need to be more careful," or "How could you be so clumsy?" But behind the words there may be a more self-oriented reaction: "Why should your clumsiness make me late for work or mess up my table or..." In other words, "How could you do this to me?" Anger is a self-centered reaction to inconvenience or disappointment.

In perfect contrast to our egocentric humanness, is Jesus' graciousness. His focus was always on those around him. He was, and is, totally tuned to our needs and our ways of seeing the world. Based on his discernment of us, he acts to bless us.

If we follow his example, we might respond to spilt milk in gracious ways: "Oops. The milk spilled. I'll grab you a towel," or "Too bad. We all spill sometimes," or "Cool! I have wanted to do milk painting on the table for a long time. What shall we draw?"

When we act with the child's needs in mind, we act very differently. When we understand that our children are doing the best they know how in a big, confusing world in which they often feel awkward and powerless, we, like Jesus, can act redemptively. When a child falls short because of lack of wisdom or experience, we can teach rather than punish.

I love the compassion in a statement by Jeffrey R. Holland:

> When a battered, weary swimmer tries valiantly to get back to shore, after having fought strong winds and rough waves which he should never have challenged in the first place, those of us who might have had better judgment, or perhaps just better luck, ought not to row out to his side, beat him with our oars, and shove his head back underwater. That's not what boats were made for. But some of us do that to each other.[19]

---

19 Jeffrey R. Holland, *However Long and Hard the Road* (Salt Lake City: Deseret Book, 1985), 71.

More than we realize, our anger hurts and frightens our children. It is much like clubbing them with oars. God recommends different behavior:

> And ye will not suffer your children that they go hungry, or naked; neither will ye suffer that they transgress the laws of God, and fight and quarrel one with another, and serve the devil, who is the master of sin, or who is the evil spirit which hath been spoken of by our fathers, he being an enemy to all righteousness. (Mosiah 4:14)

We do not teach our children to avoid fighting and quarrelling by fighting and quarrelling with them. We recall God's counsel: "And, ye fathers, *provoke not your children to wrath*: but bring them up in the nurture and admonition of the Lord" (Ephesians 6:4, emphasis added).

Anger is addictive. A couple of marriage scholars have described the satisfaction of having someone to blame:

> How wonderful to have someone to blame! How wonderful to live with one's nemesis! You may be miserable, but you feel forever in the right. You may be fragmented, but you feel absolved of all the blame for it.[20]

Apparently this is the way Cain felt after he killed his brother: "And Cain gloried in that which he had done, saying: I am free; surely the flocks of my brother falleth into my hands" (Moses 5:33).

In some sense, Cain was free; free as a fugitive and a vagabond. The natural man, unchanged by the Spirit of God, experiences many such empty victories. Does one feel better after delivering punishment? Can there ever be enough punishment? Does wrestling a foe into submission bring peace?

---

20 A. Christensen and N. S. Jacobson, *Reconcilable Differences* (New York: Guilford, 2000), 17.

Or are hate and envy addictive? Does Satan laugh when he gets us swept up in battering each other with our rightness?

Let's return to Buechner's observation. At the beginning of this section we quoted him describing anger as a feast fit for a king. He finishes his observation with the following words: "The chief drawback is that what you are wolfing down is yourself. The skeleton at the feast is you."[21]

Anger can destroy us and our families. God invites us to turn away wrath and be soft-spoken parents.

The Science of Anger

Research has shown that hostility can damage our hearts. Those who are angry, are five times as likely to have serious heart problems as those who aren't. Anger is bad for the heart! In fact, "hostility [is] a strong predictor of mortality rate—death from all causes combined."[22]

There are three parts to the anger that destroys us: cynical mistrust of others, frequent angry feelings, and aggressive behavior. For example, if a person is following you too closely when you are driving your car, you may at first wonder if they are stupid, then you may feel angry, then perhaps you will act to spite them by deliberately slowing down. All the while, you are damaging your own heart.

The same thing happens in our relationships with our children. We may find that they have not washed the dishes or done their homework. We may find that they have picked on a younger brother or sister.

---

21 Frederick Buechner, *Wishful Thinking* (San Fransisco: Harper & Row, 1993), 2.
22 Carol Tavris, *Anger: The Misunderstood Emotion* (New York: Simon and Schuster, 1983), 123.

Our first reaction is cynicism: "That is a lazy kid," "I knew I couldn't trust him," "That kid never thinks of anyone but himself!"

And we get angry. We feel indignant. We want to punish the child. (Any time we are inclined to hurt someone, we should question the impulse. God declares that vengeance belongs only to him.)

Then we get aggressive. The aggression may be verbal or physical. We may lecture or yell at children. We may spank them, shove them, or drag them to their rooms.

All of this is bad for our heart. And it is bad for our relationships. As therapist Bernie Zilbergeld said about anger in marriage: "I cannot count the number of times that married couples tell me: 'I've got all this anger bottled up and I need to get it out.' Sure you do, and I'll be happy to cater the divorce."[23]

As Carol Tavris has observed in her classic book on anger, "Most of the time, expressing anger makes people angrier, solidifies an angry attitude, and establishes a hostile habit. If you keep quiet about momentary irritations and distract yourself with pleasant activity until your fury simmers down, chances are you will feel better, and feel better faster, than if you let yourself go in a shouting match."[24]

The mixed blessing of focus

Anger has a way of focusing—even narrowing—our attention. This may be very useful if we are preparing to fight off attacking wolves or marauding bandits. In those situations, the focus can be very helpful. It

---

23 Carol Tavris, *Anger: The Misunderstood Emotion* (New York: Simon and Schuster, 1983), 247.
24 Carol Tavris, *Anger: The Misunderstood Emotion* (New York: Simon and Schuster, 1983), 159.

allows us to put all our resources and extraordinary energy into the service of defending ourselves.

That same focus is entirely unhelpful if you are dealing with family members who spilled the milk or came home late. In those cases, the focus may over-energize an aggressive attack. Rather than think of the misdeeds as assaults on us or heaven, it is more helpful to think of the misdeeds in the context of the children's histories, intentions, and circumstances.

Returning again to Tavris: "Because anger is fomented, maintained, and inflamed by the statements we make to ourselves and others when we are provoked ('What a thoughtless lout!' 'Who does she think she is!'), [we can learn] to control anger the same way, by reinterpreting the supposed provocation: 'Maybe he's having a rough day'; 'She must be very unhappy if she would do such a thing.' This is what people who are slow to anger do naturally: They empathize with the other person's behavior and try to find justifications for it."[25]

When we are tempted to be angry with a child, we can apply compassion. We can try to see the world through their less-experienced eyes. We can try to understand their life, challenges, and personality. In fact, there are many things we can do to turn away wrath.

The Soft-Spoken Parent

You may or may not believe that anger is a problem for you. But let's imagine your family using better ways of preventing, managing, and overcoming conflict.

First let's imagine that you have strengthened relationships so that most of the time family members enjoy each other. Little complaints don't become

---

25 Carol Tavris, *Anger: The Misunderstood Emotion* (New York: Simon and Schuster, 1983), 290.

big battles. Family members laugh, work, and play together feeling safe, loving, and affectionate. Imagine that family members feel this way most of the time. That is prevention!

Second, let's imagine that you have good ways of dealing with those power-surges of anger that catch you unawares. Maybe you've learned ways of thinking differently about the irritations in family life. Maybe you've learned ways to delay or respond positively to feelings of anger. But, instead of getting dragged to foolishness by strong feelings, you have learned to take charge of them. You have learned how to make peace and consideration the themes of your parenting.

Third, let's imagine that you have learned good ways of slowing down anger that has gotten started or making repairs when your temper has gotten the best of you. Picture your family without the pains of extended resentful silences. Picture your family quickly pushing anger and evil out the back door and throwing open the windows to light, warmth, and love.

Anger should be as rare a visitor to our homes as the appliance repairman. Anger does happen, but peace, cooperation, and appreciation can be the central features of our family life.

Imagining a better family life does not make it better automatically. But it provides vision and purpose for our efforts. And it is far better than ruminating over a long history of brush fires.

So imagine your family as a lovely garden filled with brilliant blooms, gentle breezes, warm sunshine, singing birds, and peaceful repose. There may be an occasional mosquito seeking a victim, but you rejoice in the blessing of loving relationships.

May it be so for you and for all of us.

Process of Change

As you study the 55 strategies for turning away wrath, remember that some things we can do will help us change for the better. However, some things—even done with the best of intentions—will actually make things worse.

For example, inventorying mistakes and failures may evoke negative feelings and reactions. Carrying around a burden of guilt does not help us travel better. However, recognizing our mistakes will help us if it sends us to the great Repairman of souls.

> And if men come unto me I will show unto them their weakness. I give unto men weakness that they may be humble; and *my grace is sufficient for all men that humble themselves before me*; for if they humble themselves before me, and have faith in me, *then will I make weak things become strong unto me*. (Ether 12:27, emphasis added)

As I understand it, God's counsel on change suggests that we should be humble, recognizing our dependence on him with any progress we make. While we never stop trying, we always recognize our dependence upon his help.

Then we celebrate our victories. We thank Heavenly Father every time we do better than we might have done.

There is another key to change. Each of us has different God-given gifts. (See the amazing 46th section of the Doctrine and Covenants for more about gifts.) Some of the strategies described below will fit you wonderfully well. Others will not. It is important for us, as parents, to put our energy into those that fit us.

When we are inspired by an idea that could help us, we might profitably pre-experience our response. We can think through a typical blow-up and plan what we will say and how we will act the next time this blow-up occurs. We might even plan what we will do with the unhelpful feelings that inevitably arise. It might be helpful to write out the plan or to pre-imagine it several times so that we are ready when the crisis arises.

Finally, thank Heaven for repentance! We will all fluff it many times. Yet the victory of a peaceful family will go to those who are determined to keep bringing healing goodness and wisdom to their family life. We should be as patient with our own learning process as an ideal parent would be—or as the Ideal Parent actually is!

May God bless you and your family with peace.

The 55 Strategies

1. Get your heart right.

Have you ever felt so serene and peaceful that you loved the whole world?

I remember as a young missionary in Ocala, Florida, being asked to bless the sacrament one Sunday in fast meeting. I don't remember the details of that morning. But I know that my companion and I sang the sacrament hymn while we broke the bread. I remember that I was filled with love, joy, and peace.

When we sat while the sacrament was passed, I looked over the people of that little ward. I had been in Ocala long enough to know some of the eccentricities and weaknesses in the ward. But, filled with the Spirit, I loved them all. I felt that I wanted to embrace them and bless them in any way I could. Their weaknesses and unkindnesses meant nothing to me. I simply loved them.

I suppose that what I felt was charity, the pure love that comes as a gift from Christ. To be able to see as he sees, feel as he feels, and love as he loves is a blessed experience. If all of us were filled with charity all the time, anger would not be a problem.

But we are not and it is. Most of the time we operate between mild irritation and total annoyance. That is part of living in a telestial world where thorn and thistle (as well as children and co-workers) torment and afflict us.

So the blessed state of charity does not come to us regularly or easily. But, just as with the long-awaited trip to Disneyland, we should not lose sight of the goal. It may take years of patient preparation, but we should not settle for an hour at Chuck E. Cheese's. We were meant for better things.

So any process that keeps our hearts tender, compassionate, and long-suffering should be cherished.

Reflection:

Think of a time when you have had your heart right.
How did it feel? _____

_____

_____

What helped you get there? _____

_____

_____

How can you get there again? _____

_____

_____

How can you make that experience more common for you?_____

_____

_____

Applying this strategy:

☐ I ask Father for help.
☐ I remember (with gratitude) past successes with this strategy.
☐ I ask myself, does this strategy fit me? If not, can I adapt it or should I discard it?
☐ I plan my response for next time the challenge arises.
☐ I imagine or pre-experience the better way of responding.
☐ I try it out.
☐ I keep refining my efforts—otherwise known as repenting.

Get your heart right.

Notes on my progress: _____

_____

_____

_____

_____

_____

_____

2. Just say "no" to anger.

Anger makes a lot of bold claims that it can't support. It claims to represent some reality when in fact it represents a bold misunderstanding. The misunderstanding that undergirds anger is the belief that my way is the right way and when you deviate from it, you're messed up. There's actually another misunderstanding in anger—that chewing people out causes them to behave better.

Jesus taught the people powerfully and poetically when he visited the Americas:

> "For verily, verily I say unto you, He that hath the spirit of contention is not of me, but is of the devil, who is the father of contention, and he stirreth up the hearts of men to contend with anger, one with another. Behold, this is not my doctrine, to stir up the hearts of men with anger, one against another; but this is my doctrine, that such things should be done away." (3 Nephi 11:29–30)

Jesus does not provide any philosophy or rationale for this commandment. He simply commands us to shun contention. In a following verse, he tells us that "the Father commandeth all men, everywhere, to repent and believe in [him]" (3 Nephi 11:32).

Jesus commands us to avoid contention. There are times when we will simply choose peace over controversy. Simple obedience is a good basis for good behavior.

Of course when our hearts are changed and perfected, good behavior will be our natural disposition. Between simple obedience and changed hearts, there are many things we can do to curb our wrath.

Every tool we can use to shape our minds, hearts, and behavior closer to the Divine is all good.

Reflection:

Think of a time when you just said "no" to anger.

How did it feel? _____

_____

_____

What helped you get there? _____

_____

_____

How can you get there again? _____

_____

_____

How can you make that experience more common for you? _____

_____

_____

Applying this strategy:

☐ I ask Father for help.

☐ I remember (with gratitude) past successes with this strategy.

☐ I ask myself, does this strategy fit me? If not, can I adapt it or should I discard it?

☐ I plan my response for next time the challenge arises.

☐ I imagine or pre-experience the better way of responding.

☐ I try it out.

☐ I keep refining my efforts—otherwise known as repenting.

Notes on my progress: _____

_____

_____

_____

_____

_____

_____

3. Choose laughter over accusation.

Some years ago when our children were small, I found that the previous user of the bathroom had finished a roll of toilet paper without replacing it. Unfortunately, I discovered this at an inopportune time. I felt like launching a full-scale investigation and then punishing the perpetrator. I was angry.

But something inside me whispered that there was a better way. How could I accuse and humiliate the people I loved most?

So I called the whole family—all five of us—together into the small bathroom. Then I announced that we had a serious problem. Someone had finished the roll of paper without replacing it. So we would be instituting a new policy. All toilet paper would be stored in a locked shed in the hallway. Paper would only be issued after completing a form in triplicate accounting for each square of paper that was requested. .

The children laughed at me. I laughed at me. They got the point without any investigation, accusation, or rancor. Truly "a soft answer turneth away wrath" (Proverbs 15:1). So do squiggly—or humorous—answers.

Very often we want to help our children act better, but then we often set a terrible example of immature rant. Surely there is a better way. Often, humor is not a bad substitute for anger—as long as no one is hurt or humiliated.

I read a story of a teenager who had just learned to drive. She regularly begged for opportunities to drive the family. Once, during a family vacation, her father allowed her to drive on a long, straight stretch of highway. She was in heaven…until. Suddenly there was a turn in the road. Caught by surprise, she swung too wide and ran into a service station's sign. She stopped the car and braced herself for a lecture.

Her father, always mindful of his children's feelings, was quiet for some time. Then he turned to the rest of the family in the backseat and said, "As long as we're stopped here, does anybody need to use the rest room?" I suspect that this teenager loved her father for his kindness.

It is important that family laughter not be corrosive or sarcastic. We must never laugh at a family member's pain. But there will be times when laughing together will help the family draw closer together. Kindness and happiness are the lubricants of positive family life.

Reflection:

Think of a time when you have used humor instead of anger.
How did it feel? _____

_____

_____

What helped you get there? _____

_____

_____

How can you get there again? _____

_____

_____

How can you make that experience more common for you?_____

_____

_____

Applying this strategy:

☐ I ask Father for help.
☐ I remember (with gratitude) past successes with this strategy.
☐ I ask myself, does this strategy fit me? If not, can I adapt it or should I discard it?

Choose laughter over accusation.

☐ I plan my response for next time the challenge arises.

☐ I imagine or pre-experience the better way of responding.

☐ I try it out.

☐ I keep refining my efforts—otherwise known as repenting.

Notes on my progress: _____

_____

_____

_____

_____

_____

_____

4. Look into the child's heart.

Very often we judge children's behaviors based on their effects on us. If their actions (or inactions) irritate me, then the children are malicious—or at least careless and irresponsible.

This is much like blaming my extra weight on the fat calories in Reese's peanut butter cups. How much sense would it make to sue the manufacturers of Reese's for making their candy too delectable? Their recipe is not a carefully devised conspiracy against my weight. It is my lack of moderation that is my enemy.

Likewise when a child forgets to close the door, turn off the lights, or to keep cookies out of the living room, they are generally not making a concerted effort to make us poor or crazy. They are probably being children. (By the way, do we sometimes take cookies in the living room—hoping not to get caught?)

Children's motives are much like ours—only probably a little purer. They are trying to find ways to get their needs met and enjoy life. They probably even want to do what's right as much as they can.

Sometimes their mistakes are simply the result of not knowing better, or being tired, or feeling thwarted and frustrated. To treat them harshly for their humanness is counterproductive.

So the wrath we aim at them is probably unnecessary and unhelpful. We can scald them with our unhappiness and we will all be the poorer.

When Elder Holland was president of BYU he told a poignant story of overreaction.

Early in our married life my young family and I were laboring through graduate school at a university in New England. I was going to school full-time and teaching half-time. We had two small children then, with little money and lots of pressures.

One evening I came home from long hours at school, feeling the weight of the world on my shoulders. Everything seemed to be especially demanding and discouraging and dark. I wondered if the dawn would ever come. Then, as I walked into our small student apartment, there was an unusual silence in the room.

"What's the trouble?" I asked.

"Matthew has something he wants to tell you," my wife said.

"Matt, what do you have to tell me?" He was quietly playing with his toys in the corner of the room, trying very hard not to hear me. "Matt," I said a little louder, "do you have something to tell me?"

He stopped playing, but for a moment didn't look up. Then these two enormous, tear-filled brown eyes turned toward me, and with the pain only a five-year-old can know, he said, "I didn't mind Mommy tonight, and I spoke back to her." With that he burst into tears, and his entire little body shook with grief. A childish mistake had been noted, a painful confession had been offered, the growth of a five-year-old was continuing, and loving peace could have been wonderfully underway.

Everything might have been just terrific—except for me. If you can imagine such an idiotic thing, I lost my temper. It wasn't that I lost it with Matt—it was with a hundred and one other things on my mind; but he didn't know that, and I wasn't disciplined enough to admit it. He got the whole load of bricks.

I told him how disappointed I was and how much more I thought I could have expected from him. Then I did what I had never done before in his life—I told him that he was to go straight to bed and that I would not be in to say his prayers with him or to tell him a bedtime story. Muffling his sobs, he obediently went to his bedside, where he knelt—alone—to say his prayers. Then he stained his little pillow with tears his father should have been wiping away.[26]

When we know we are tired, we should be especially cautious about our reactions—and over-reactions. In all cases we should look on children not as annoying little people who are tormenting us deliberately, but as children who are doing the best they know how to do.

Reflection:

Think of a time when you have looked into your child's heart and intentions.

How did it feel? _____

_____

_____

What helped you get there? _____

_____

_____

---

26 Jeffrey R. Holland, "Within the Clasp of Your Arms," *Ensign*, May 1983, 37.

How can you get there again? _____

_____

_____

How can you make that experience more common for you?_____

_____

_____

Applying this strategy:

☐ I ask Father for help.

☐ I remember (with gratitude) past successes with this strategy.

☐ I ask myself, does this strategy fit me? If not, can I adapt it or should I discard it?

☐ I plan my response for next time the challenge arises.

☐ I imagine or pre-experience the better way of responding.

☐ I try it out.

☐ I keep refining my efforts—otherwise known as repenting.

Notes on my progress: _____

_____

_____

_____

_____

_____

_____

5. Look on them with compassion.

We can remove wrath from family relationships by looking on each other with compassion. Brigham Young taught us to apply compassion to our perception of weakness:

> Let all Latter-day Saints learn that the weaknesses of their brethren are not sins. When men or women [or children] undesignedly commit a wrong, do not attribute that to them as a sin. Let us learn to be compassionate one with another; let mercy and kindness soften every angry and fretful temper, that we may become long-suffering and beneficial in all our communications one with another.[27]

When our daughter Emily was in kindergarten, she and a neighbor friend named Donna often went across the street to the school playground to kick a ball and swing. One day as the two girls left our house and headed to the playground, Emily stopped at curbside and Donna dashed into the street. A slow-moving car was unable to stop and hit Donna sending her skidding and finally sprawling on the pavement. She laid in the street frightened and pained.

What is the right response to Donna's pain? Would it make sense to approach her and remind her of our oft-repeated and wise counsel to look both ways before crossing the street? Would it make sense to tell her that maybe she needed a timeout to reflect on her carelessness? Would we ground her or demand that she apologize to the frightened driver?

No! Such callousness is akin to abuse. We would go to Donna and offer words of love and assurance even as we helped her get comfortable. We

---

27 *Discourses of Brigham Young*, ed. John A. Widtsoe (Salt Lake City: Deseret Book, 1954), 273.

would call for appropriate medical care. We would do anything we could to help her feel safe and to start the healing process.

Far more often than we realize, our children are injured by painful encounters with life. They come home bruised, skinned, and bleeding. We adults almost surely do not realize how often they feel frightened and wounded. If we try to understand their pains and challenges, we are likely to look upon them with compassion rather than judgment and impatience.

Time and again Jesus encountered people with various maladies. The New Testament reports that he responded with compassion to the blind, possessed, bereaved, injured, and those who were reluctantly repenting.

In Jesus' great story of the good Samaritan, he contrasts the official response of priest and Levite (who walked around the injured one) with that of a true neighbor: "When he saw him, he had compassion."

He had compassion! It is the difference between responding in the world's way and responding in the Lord's way. It is the mark of the Christ-like soul.

When our children are injured by unkind words from classmates, rejection by friends, stinging criticism from teachers—whatever the source of the injury—we can respond with compassion.

Jesus is the perfect example. After he had ransomed our souls by paying for our sins, he went the extra mile. He bore our pains, discomforts, and disappointments so that he would fully understand us (Alma 7:11–12).

Amazing! We can never rightly say to him, "You just don't understand how I feel." He does understand! And he paid a terrible price so that he could understand everything from the agony of psoriasis to the pains of childbirth. He knows what it is like to be shunned and hated. He has personally experienced in Gethsemane the pains of divorce and the agony of cancer. There is no pain we will ever experience that he has not borne—so that he can respond with compassion to every pain we ever bear.

And he invites us to look on each other with compassion. Enoch was surprised to find that God wept as he witnessed the suffering of his wicked children—even though they deserved to suffer (Moses 7:33). He questioned God about it. God responded: "These thy brethren...are the workmanship of my hands.... Should not the heavens weep, seeing these shall suffer?" (Moses 7:32, 37).

God hates suffering even when it is suffering that we have brought upon ourselves. He looks on our struggles and suffering with compassion.

When we see one of our children burdened or injured—even if it is due to their own foolishness—we do not ask, "What's wrong with you, Sourpuss?" Instead, we approach with compassion in our words and in our spirit: "Looks like you've had a hard day." We lean into their struggle with our love.

We do not demand that they tell us more than they are ready to share. But we try to remember and be humbled by the challenges of being a child—feeling unskilled and often powerless. We come to them with emotional first aid.

Having compassion on them can prevent us from attacking unhelpfully. It can also help us deal with differences and irritations when we have them. And it can make us more willing repenters when we have added insult to their injuries.

Reflection:

Think of a time when you have looked on your children with compassion. How did it feel? _____

_____

_____

What helped you get there? _____

_____

_____

How can you get there again? _____

_____

_____

How can you make that experience more common for you?_____

_____

_____

Applying this strategy:

☐ I ask Father for help.

☐ I remember (with gratitude) past successes with this strategy.

☐ I ask myself, does this strategy fit me? If not, can I adapt it or should I discard it?

☐ I plan my response for next time the challenge arises.

☐ I imagine or pre-experience the better way of responding.

☐ I try it out.

☐ I keep refining my efforts—otherwise known as repenting.

Notes on my progress: _____

_____

_____

_____

_____

_____

_____

6. Listen to their hearts.

When children are struggling with burdens of pain, we are likely to jump in with unhelpful advising. We may even get angry at the behaviors that got them in their fixes. There is a better way to help them heal, honor their agency, and help them learn. One of the most important things we can do is listen with our hearts.

As children are dealing with disappointment or despair, we bring our compassion as an offering. We show our love and dedication by listening with our souls.

For example, if my son gets into trouble at school, I can try to feel what that experience was like for him. And I can say, "Ouch! What a terrible experience!" In response to every comment he makes, I can try to offer words that show compassion, understanding, and caring.

Another example: if my daughter is hurt by the cruelty of a friend, I might respond, "Oh, Darling! That must feel awful!" Then I stop to listen to anything else she wants to say.

The common parental temptation is to say far too much—to tell about our pains or to give advice. But a good doctor does not start telling about his own bike accidents or start encouraging his patient to be more careful. He focuses on the patient's injury.

Likewise, our focus on the pain cleanses the wound and begins the healing process. Can you think of a time when someone has responded to your pain with words of compassion?

I remember when I was a young school teacher and my father asked me how my teaching was going. I unloaded on him the demands of preparing many subjects, the pressures from administrators and parents, as well as the impossibility of managing so many students. When I finished, I expected my father to say, "What you need to do is…" But he didn't. Instead he said with heartfelt compassion, "That must be overwhelming." That was all he said. But I still feel the warmth of his compassion. Dad listened to my heart and offered his compassion as an offering.

He gave me that unique gift of empathy. Maybe the gift is powerful in part because it is so rare. Maybe it is powerful because it requires the giver to set aside his own agenda, feelings, and history in order to inhabit the experience of another person.

If we want to help our children learn to settle themselves from feelings of wrath, we can listen with our hearts. It is far more effective than giving formulaic advice or demanding that they settle down. It is a great gift of love.

Haim Ginott, the great psychologist, tells of a parent who takes his child for ice cream. When asked which flavor he wanted, he replied, "I want a scoop of every flavor!" This response could tempt any parent to get angry: "Why, you spoiled brat! I offer you a cone and you want the whole creamery!"

The attack would not be helpful. Instead, the parent can listen to his heart. "Wouldn't that be great! Wouldn't you love to have some of every single flavor! Which two flavors would you like to have today?" The limit can be delivered with loving empathy.

Reflection:

Think of a time when you have had listened to your child's heart. How did it feel? _____

_____

_____

What helped you get there? _____

_____

_____

How can you get there again? _____

_____

_____

How can you make that experience more common for you?_____

_____

_____

Applying this strategy:

- ☐ I ask Father for help.
- ☐ I remember (with gratitude) past successes with this strategy.
- ☐ I ask myself, does this strategy fit me? If not, can I adapt it or should I discard it?
- ☐ I plan my response for next time the challenge arises.
- ☐ I imagine or pre-experience the better way of responding.
- ☐ I try it out.
- ☐ I keep refining my efforts—otherwise known as repenting.

Notes on my progress: _____

_____

_____

_____

_____

_____

_____

7. Choose peace.

God teaches surprising lessons about dealing with injustice. For example, after suffering terrible injustices, Joseph Smith cried out to Heaven for vengeance on the Missourians. "Let thine anger be kindled against our enemies; and, in the fury of thine heart, with they sword avenge us of our wrongs" (D&C 121:5).

The Lord gave the perfect instructions for dealing with injustice: "My son, peace be unto thy soul; thine adversity and thine afflictions shall be but a small moment; And then, if thou endure it well, God shall exalt thee on high; thou shalt triumph over all thy foes" (D&C 121: 7–8).

When we are upset with one of our boys, we may get a total eclipse of our son (and his Son). We may think of nothing but re-balancing the scales of justice. We volunteer to join God in smiting wickedness. It's not a pretty sight.

Remember that God has asked us to leave judging and punishing to One who is perfect (Mormon 8:20). That pretty effectively excludes us. It even excluded Joseph Smith. God's response to Joseph's wrath was twofold: Choose peace. Keep the eternal perspective.

When we truly trust God, the tempests on the ocean of life do not overwhelm us. We know Who commands the waves to be still. We trust him.

We trust him to help our children develop good character in a world that promotes evil. We trust him to calm the waves in our own souls. We trust him to help us find the right way to teach our children. But we cannot do that when we have grabbed the reigns of the universe from him and are enthusiastically handing out judgment and vengeance.

We are much less likely to overreact when we remember Who is in charge of the human family. In times of tempest, we would do well to think of him. As we do, we might even hear his words in our souls: "Peace, be still."

There will need to be both nurture and admonition—love and counsel—still ahead. It is good to remember that our action grows from the peace in our own soul.

A mother once asked me what she should do about her 4-year-old daughter who had scratched a neighbor's child. The mother wanted to be sure that her daughter got the message: "Your behavior is not acceptable." I asked for more information about the incident. The 4-year-old had been playing with her 6-year-old sister and the sister's friend while Mom was preparing dinner. (A sensitive parent sees trouble coming already. Older children are often not very gracious toward younger children who want to play with them.)

As they were playing, the younger child got upset and scratched her sister's friend. I asked the mother how she dealt with it. "I scratched my little girl and then I locked her in her room and told her she could not come out for three days." The mother explained, "I wanted her to learn a lesson."

I think the little girl learned a lesson—but probably not the one Mom intended. It was noteworthy that the mother had not mentioned the stresses in their family life that may have impacted the girl's behavior. The dad was overwhelmed with a work project and was working long hours. Mom had started a new job with new pressures and extra hours for training. To accommodate her mother's schedule, the little girl had been moved to a new child care center where she had no friends. And, at the time of the incident, the girls were hungry and tired.

None of these factors justify scratching. But they help us understand the little girl. I asked the mom if her girl scratched often. "No. Maybe once before." When the mother asked me what she might have done differently, I suggested that the little girl probably needed help finding other ways to express her frustration. In fact, Mom might help her self-soothe by sitting with her little girl in a rocking chair and getting herself calm even as she calmed her little girl. When both were peaceful, Mom might offer understanding and help her daughter learn new ways.

"You must have been very upset today." Mom listens and empathizes. "What a hard day! Did the scratching help you get what you wanted?" Mom listens some more. "Is there anything you could have done differently?" Mom coaches her girl to better ways.

Peace is a better setting for learning than anger is.

Reflection:

Think of a time when you have chosen peace.
How did it feel? _____

_____

_____

What helped you get there? _____

_____

_____

How can you get there again? _____

_____

_____

How can you make that experience more common for you? _____

_____

_____

Applying this strategy:

☐ I ask Father for help.

☐ I remember (with gratitude) past successes with this strategy.

☐ I ask myself, does this strategy fit me? If not, can I adapt it or should I discard it?

☐ I plan my response for next time the challenge arises.

☐ I imagine or pre-experience the better way of responding.

☐ I try it out.

☐ I keep refining my efforts—otherwise known as repenting.

Notes on my progress: _____

_____

_____

_____

_____

_____

_____

8. Get their side of the story.

On one occasion we were planning to go visit a friend who had suffered some major setbacks. We had an appointment to visit as a family. So we made a point of telling the children to be home at a specific time. We were quite emphatic.

But at the appointed time, Emily was missing and could not be found. She had gone to play with Betsy, but the two girls had gone on a walk and had not returned. As we waited at home, I stewed. I reflected on other times that Emily had been late. I fretted that we would not be able to visit our friend as a whole family. I built quite a case. Emily's carelessness had robbed us of an important opportunity as a family.

The rest of us went to visit the friend. When we returned home, Emily was there looking very sheepish. My tirade was well-prepared and fully-rehearsed. Fortunately, I had just enough good sense to ask Emily to explain her absence at the appointed time.

She apologized. She said that she and Betsy had gone to see Millie Haws, a widow who lived down the street. They had visited for a while and then told Millie that they needed to go. But Millie begged them to hear just one more story. They fidgeted and fretted but did not know how to break free from Millie's story in a polite way.

I might have lectured Emily about assertiveness and responsibility, but I, like her, had been caught more than once in Millie's magical story-telling. All I could do was sigh in sympathy and thank Emily for the compassion that took her to visit Millie in the first place.

Each of us constructs stories to explain what we see others do. We take what we know of the facts and personalities and we put them together in a coherent manner. There is only one problem. There are vast gaps in our knowledge of facts and our assessments of other people's character. That is why it is so important to forego dogmatism in favor of humility. That is why it is so important to hear their side of the story. "It is a mighty thin pancake that does not have two sides," said Mary Christensen.[28]

Reflection:

Think of a time when you have gotten their side of the story.
How did it feel? _____

_____

_____

What helped you get there? _____

_____

_____

How can you get there again? _____

_____

_____

How can you make that experience more common for you?_____

_____

_____

Applying this strategy:

☐ I ask Father for help.

☐ I remember (with gratitude) past successes with this strategy.

☐ I ask myself, does this strategy fit me? If not, can I adapt it or should I discard it?

---

28 Mary Christensen, "BYU Today," *BYU Magazine*, December 1984, 4.

Get their side of the story.

☐ I plan my response for next time the challenge arises.
☐ I imagine or pre-experience the better way of responding.
☐ I try it out.
☐ I keep refining my efforts—otherwise known as repenting.

Notes on my progress: _____

_____

_____

_____

_____

_____

_____

9. Walk in their shoes.

It is very hard for adults to understand what life is like for children. We have changed so slowly and so completely from childhood to adulthood that we may not even realize how different our experience is from theirs.

For example, we might not guess that prominent among children's concerns is the dread that they might wet their pants in school? That might seem silly to adults. But maybe we forget that they must get permission to go to the restroom. They, on the other hand, can remember times when they have had accidents. And they remember the humiliation of being teased over those accidents. Children often feel quite powerless in their lives.

Most of us have forgotten many of the challenges of adolescence. Teens are just learning to think about thinking. They are learning to think about how other people think about them. It can be a very confusing—albeit necessary—development.

We sometimes talk about adolescent egocentrisms. For example, teens tend to feel as if people are watching them. They also yearn to be heroic. And they often believe that they are invincible. As a result of these ways of thinking, teens may be very sensitive and they make take inordinate time getting ready for school. And they may ruminate about things that their classmates say to them or about them.

It may seem to adults that teens are irrational and oversensitive. But this stage of making sense of their inner world and their social world is as important as a 1-year-old learning to walk or a 2-year-old stringing words together to express ideas. It is a normal and important part of development.

Do you remember feeling painfully self-conscious as a child? Do you remember wondering what people thought of you? Do you remember blushing with embarrassment over things you said? Do you remember being made fun of by classmates? If so, you may have the humility to understand your child.

Of course our children are different from us in important ways. So, our experiences only provide us needed humility; they do not give us the answers for our children's challenges.

With humility in place, we can study our children. We can notice what they love and what they are afraid of. We can notice what they enjoy and what they dread. Our objective is to walk in their shoes so that we can better understand their view of the world. If we do this with genuine humility, we can then help them navigate in their lives.

Nancy and I used to go out to dinner occasionally so that we could discuss each of our children. Nancy would ask how we might help one child make more friends or deal with a difficult experience. I offered possibilities. She knew which ones fitted them best. She saw things I did not because she spent so much time with them and because she is such a good listener.

Anjelica Huston reports that, when she was young, she made some negative comment about Vincent van Gogh at the dinner table. She said somewhat flippantly that she didn't like his work. Her father, the famous movie director John Huston, exploded: "You don't like van Gogh? Then name six of his paintings and tell me why you don't like them." When she couldn't, he commanded her: "Leave the room, and until you know what you're talking about, don't come back with your opinions to the dinner table."

Harsh attacks do not humble and they do not inform. They create resentment. John Huston might have considered forms of art he didn't enjoy. Then he might understand that van Gogh did not speak to his daughter. Contrast Huston's harsh response with the teaching response described by Haim Ginott:

> When Clara, age fourteen, criticized modern painting, mother did not dispute her opinion. Nor did she condemn her taste.
>
> Mother: You don't like abstract art?
> Clara: I sure don't. It's ugly.
> Mother: You prefer representational art?
> Clara: What's that?
> Mother: You like it when a house looks like a house, and a tree like a tree and a person like a person.
> Clara: Yes.
> Mother: Then you like representational art.
> Clara: Imagine that. All my life I liked representational art and didn't know it.

Clara's mother used her daughter's statement to educate her. And in the process she showed both respect and affection.

You know the old saying: We cannot understand someone until we have walked a mile in their shoes. That is certainly true of understanding our children. When we understand the landscape of their lives—their hopes, anxieties, dreams, and monsters, we are less likely to get angry or impatient with them. We are more likely to help them find their way to happy adulthoods.

Reflection:

Think of a time when you have walked in your children's shoes—when you have connected their experience with your own.

How did it feel? _____

_____

_____

What helped you get there? _____

_____

_____

How can you get there again? _____

_____

_____

How can you make that experience more common for you? _____

_____

_____

Applying this strategy:

☐ I ask Father for help.

☐ I remember (with gratitude) past successes with this strategy.

☐ I ask myself, does this strategy fit me? If not, can I adapt it or should I discard it?

☐ I plan my response for next time the challenge arises.

☐ I imagine or pre-experience the better way of responding.

☐ I try it out.

☐ I keep refining my efforts—otherwise known as repenting.

Notes on my progress: _____

_____

_____

_____

_____

_____

10. Put off 'til tomorrow what shouldn't be said today.

Sometimes a clever observation is exploding to get out of us. We're tempted to point out that our children brought their suffering on themselves because of their bad decisions. Or when they seem cocky, we're tempted to cut them down to size with a sarcastic remark. Or maybe we're mad because we've been stupid and we'd rather blame the child than take responsibility.

As the indignation surges, a voice inside of us gently reminds us that we should not make our terse observation. As the saying goes, it is never a good idea to burn a cathedral just to fry an egg—even when we are terribly hungry. To torch a relationship in order to feel clever or exonerated is equally shortsighted.

Torn between the temptation to correct/level/humble the child and the invitation to kindness and helpfulness, many of us gag the angel and speak for the devil. That's where the impulsive energy is. It is so much *easier* to do what comes naturally. (Or so it seems.)

Sometimes the devil cloaks evil in virtue by telling us it is our duty to correct error in our children. It is our job as parents to let them know when they are out of line. It can feel quite wrong to stifle that message.

I think that the Lord describes this impulse very ably when he said that "when we undertake to cover our sins, or to gratify our pride, our vain ambition, or to exercise control or dominion or compulsion upon the souls of the children of men, in any degree of unrighteousness, behold, the heavens withdraw themselves; the Spirit of the Lord is grieved; and when it is withdrawn, Amen to the priesthood or the authority of that" parent (D&C 121: 37).

A wise voice within us encourages us *not* to speak when we feel frustrated and judgmental. That is why we should often put off until tomorrow what we know we shouldn't say today. If we make an agreement with ourselves to never speak in haste or anger, we honor the angels of our better nature.

As we allow time to settle our souls, we can see the irritation in perspective. We should not call in a full armada to quell a tempest in a teapot. So, when we are calm enough and balanced enough to see our children as good people doing their best, then maybe we can be helpful.

Many years ago, as I wrestled with proper ways to correct our children, the Lord taught me an ironic principle: I only have the right to correct those I love. Any time I am feeling impatient or judgmental, I am not prepared to correct. The irony in this principle is that, when I am wholeheartedly loving my child, the urge to correct normally evaporates. Or, if there is still some need to correct, it is done in a spirit that is redemptive rather than punitive.

So, rather than let untamed correction spill out of us, we can make the resolve to hold our tongues when we are upset. Then we can use the time that is granted us to regain the heavenly perspective. When we are feeling loving and appreciative, the message we deliver is likely to be helpful. And a great number of irritations really don't need to even be discussed.

Reflection:

Think of a time when you have put off making the cutting remark.
How did it feel? _____

_____

_____

What helped you get there? _____

_____

_____

How can you get there again? _____

_____

_____

How can you make that experience more common for you?_____

_____

_____

Applying this strategy:

☐ I ask Father for help.

☐ I remember (with gratitude) past successes with this strategy.

☐ I ask myself, does this strategy fit me? If not, can I adapt it or should I discard it?

☐ I plan my response for next time the challenge arises.

☐ I imagine or pre-experience the better way of responding.

☐ I try it out.

☐ I keep refining my efforts—otherwise known as repenting.

Notes on my progress: _____

_____

_____

_____

_____

_____

11. Reprove betimes with sharpness.

When we are tempted to justify our anger at our children, we are likely to point to the scriptural directive: "Reproving betimes with sharpness, when moved upon by the Holy Ghost" (D&C 121:43). Clearly the Lord believes that there are times when reproof is necessary. Yet notice the condition: "When moved upon by the Holy Ghost"!

How often are our reproofs motivated by heavenly directive? In over three decades of parenting, I cannot think of a single time when my reproving was moved by the Holy Ghost. Not one.

Maybe some reproofs that I gave had that holy motivation and I just didn't realize it. But I doubt it. God has shown me what reproof that is motivated by the Spirit feels like.

There was a time when I was serving as a bishop and I realized that some fully active families in our ward had not signed up for tithing settlement. But I felt a calm indignation. It was an extraordinary sensation. As part of the announcements in sacrament meeting I mentioned the fact that some people had not signed up for settlement. I felt great power but I spoke with perfect calmness. I knew this was not a personal snit. This was a message from Heaven for which I was merely the carrier. Incidentally, all the identified families signed up right after sacrament meeting.

I have never had quite the same experience in parenting. I have often lectured, snapped, retorted, and reproved. But I know that those were expressions of my own irritation rather than messages from our perfectly loving Father.

We should note that there is a second condition placed on our reproving. Not only must it be directed by the Holy Ghost, but we must be willing to show "forth afterwards an increase of love toward him whom thou hast reproved, lest he esteem thee to be his enemy; That he may know that thy faithfulness is stronger than the cords of death" (D&C 121:43–44).

I may correct my child when moved upon by the Holy Ghost *and* when my love is so strong and evident that the child knows that I would gladly die to redeem his or her soul.

So I stand ready to reprove my children with sharpness—if I ever meet the two conditions. This is not likely to be a common experience. Rather, the general rule is to influence "by persuasion, long-suffering, by gentleness and meekness, and by love unfeigned. By kindness, and pure knowledge, which shall greatly enlarge the soul without hypocrisy, and without guile" (D&C 121:41–42). But if the time comes to correct or reprove, I am ready.

Reflection:

Think of a time when you have reproved under the influence of the Holy Ghost.

How did it feel? _____

_____

_____

What helped you get there? _____

_____

_____

How can you get there again? _____

_____

_____

How can you make that experience more common for you?_____

_____

_____

Applying this strategy:

☐ I ask Father for help.

☐ I remember (with gratitude) past successes with this strategy.

☐ I ask myself, does this strategy fit me? If not, can I adapt it or should I discard it?

☐ I plan my response for next time the challenge arises.

☐ I imagine or pre-experience the better way of responding.

☐ I try it out.

☐ I keep refining my efforts—otherwise known as repenting.

Notes on my progress: _____

_____

_____

_____

_____

_____

_____

12. Take a mental vacation.

When something bothers us, we humans often choose to be mad. We choose recreational anger. It can be quite energizing to feel that something is wrong and we should do something about it.

Research on close relationships shows that taking time-out from our fights is not useful *if* we keep up our distress-maintaining cognitions—in other words, if we keep thinking in ways that keep us mad.

If we impose a time-out on a lecture or argument with one of our children and we go out in the backyard and, while weeding the flower beds, we build our case against the child, we are not using the time-out effectively.

When we take a break from a family battle, it may be quite helpful to take a mental break as well as a physical break. We can take time to enjoy nature. We can read something edifying. Maybe we even pray. We cannot think right while feeling wrong.

The Lord has instructed us to use influence with "kindness and pure knowledge" (D&C 121:42). We have a pretty good idea of what he means by kindness. But I used to wonder what he meant by "pure knowledge." I couldn't find any commentaries on the meaning—perhaps because it should be obvious.

By "pure knowledge" I think God is saying that our thoughts about each other should be strained of mortal impurities. We should remove accusation, misunderstanding, resentment, and hostility. We should see as he sees—lovingly, compassionately, redemptively.

We cannot think right about each other when we are rehearsing each other's faults. So God directs that we see each other with kindness and pure knowledge. When we find ourselves filled with irritation or accusation, we can take a break—a mental vacation. During that break, we can fill our souls with gratitude for God's goodness, and we can seek to see each other the way God sees us.

When we return to our deliberations after our conversations with God, our exchanges are likely to be both gentler and more productive.

Reflection:

Think of a time when you have taken a mental vacation that helped you get things in perspective.

How did it feel? _____

_____

_____

What helped you get there? _____

_____

_____

How can you get there again? _____

_____

_____

How can you make that experience more common for you?_____

_____

_____

Applying this strategy:

☐ I ask Father for help.
☐ I remember (with gratitude) past successes with this strategy.

☐ I ask myself, does this strategy fit me? If not, can I adapt it or should I discard it?

☐ I plan my response for next time the challenge arises.

☐ I imagine or pre-experience the better way of responding.

☐ I try it out.

☐ I keep refining my efforts—otherwise known as repenting.

Notes on my progress: _____

_____

_____

_____

_____

_____

_____

13. Breathe deeply.

A man was guiding several youngsters through the various exhibits in a museum. He obviously was impatient with the side trips and slow pace of the children. He blurted out, "Hurry up! If you stop to look at stuff, we won't get to see anything."

The man may have needed to take a deep breath and reset his internal clock to youthful-exploration pace. If we are to be effective parents for our children, we may need to do the same.

I remember looking out my office window one day to see a mother unload her little girl from the car. As the mother rounded up her purse from the car, the little girl toddled to the sidewalk where she discovered a line of ants busily at work. I watched with interest as the mother caught up to her daughter. I expected Mom to give a cursory nod to ant watching before dragging her little girl to their appointment. She didn't. Instead Mom knelt with her girl and watched the ants. They talked about the ants. They studied the ants. For several minutes they became a team of naturalists. After several minutes, the daughter was ready to move on. That was a Mama who knew how to enjoy a breath of life.

Some people use a mindfulness of breathing as part of meditation. It can turn us from fretting to relaxing. It can help us resist anger.

But unless you meditate—or have asthma—you probably don't think about breathing very much. It just happens. We take it for granted. King Benjamin challenged us to change that:

> I say unto you, my brethren, that if you should render all the
> thanks and praise which your whole soul has power to possess, to

that God who has created you, and has kept and reserved you, and has caused that ye should rejoice, and has granted that ye should live in peace one with another—

I say unto you that if ye should serve him who has created you from the beginning, and is *preserving you from day to day, by lending you breath,* that ye may live and move and do according to your own will, and even supporting you from one moment to another—I say, if ye should serve him with all your whole souls yet ye would be unprofitable servants. (Mosiah 2:20–21, emphasis added)

Every time we inhale we might be grateful to God for the gift of life. Every time we exhale we might remember that, at our very best, we are still unprofitable servants.

Beloved King Benjamin teaches us to be grateful to God and to be humble enough to recognize our dependence on him. That is not a bad context for dealing with anger.

When we feel the rising tide of anger in our souls, we might turn our attention from organizing our complaints to enjoying each breath. Each time we inhale, we thank God for sustaining our lives. Each time we exhale, we recognize our own continuing dependence upon his merits, mercy, and grace.

William is a good example of humble gratitude. William was born with muscular dystrophy and a variety of mental diseases including schizophrenia and bipolar disorder. He had also made some mistakes that put him in jail for a time. One day Nancy and I visited him in the state mental hospital. We asked him how he was doing. He said something I'll always remember: "I can breathe—and it doesn't get any better than that."

William, with all his challenges, reminds me that I can be grateful for the simplest blessings. When I consciously thank God for the gift of breath, among a million other blessings, I'm a little less likely to dump a load of unhappiness on a struggling child.

So, let's breathe deeply.

Reflection:

Think of a time when you have taken time to relax, to breathe deeply, and to be consciously grateful.

How did it feel? _____

_____

_____

What helped you get there? _____

_____

_____

How can you get there again? _____

_____

_____

How can you make that experience more common for you?_____

_____

_____

Applying this strategy:

☐ I ask Father for help.
☐ I remember (with gratitude) past successes with this strategy.
☐ I ask myself, does this strategy fit me? If not, can I adapt it or should I discard it?
☐ I plan my response for next time the challenge arises.
☐ I imagine or pre-experience the better way of responding.

☐ I try it out.
☐ I keep refining my efforts—otherwise known as repenting.

Notes on my progress: _____

_____

_____

_____

_____

_____

_____

14. Just listen.   ❖

Most of us are like writers of fiction. We take life experience and form it into stories. But the stories are never objective. We write to make a point. We color every story with our point of view. Each of us is like a child viewing the world through a paper towel tube—or through a drinking straw.

Social psychologists have observed that we humans are not very objective—even at our best: "Instead of a naïve scientist entering the environment in search of the truth, we find the rather unflattering picture of a charlatan trying to make the data come out in a manner most advantageous to his or her already-held theories."[29]

We humans don't see very well or see very much. This seems to be Jesus' point when he talks about our inability to remove the splinter from anyone else's eyes because our vision is impaired by the thick beams in our own eyes (Matthew 7, Luke 6, 3 Nephi 14). What a graphic image! In our time, Jesus might have talked about us trying to remove an eyelash from a family member's eye while we wear a football helmet—backwards.

Jesus is not being subtle. He is making it clear: You simply cannot sort out someone else's life. The only way you can hope to make sense of someone else's experience is by removing that beam—or helmet. Unless we set aside our own assumptions, interpretations, and judgments, we cannot help a struggling child with the eyelash that troubles their vision.

If we remove our beams, and just observe, we may learn a lot. We may find that the children who have drawn our ire are just little strugglers doing the

29 S. T. Fiske and S. E. Taylor, *Social Cognition* (Reading, MA: Addison-Wesley, 1984), 88.

best they know how. They may feel confused, lonely, and sad. They may not know how to do any better.

How many times have all of us looked on friends and children and filtered their stories through our own values and expectations?

Carol Lynn Pearson shared the following experience:

> I can remember many occasions when my perception has crumbled and a glimpse inside has wiped away judgment. During my college years I looked at a fellow student, whom I will call Roy, in amazement. Where did he get such a gigantic ego? His need to be recognized and praised was never ending. Every conversation he had with anyone always centered on his recent triumphs and the projects he was now involved in that would ensure his fame. He was underappreciated and let everyone know it. His name became a joke. We had him pegged as an obnoxious egomaniac who blew his own horn from morning until night.
>
> One day I learned that one of my friends knew his family. She began to tell me some things. "Roy's father was an alcoholic. Did you know that?"
>
> "No, I didn't."
>
> "Oh, yes. He made their life just miserable. He was a crazy man. Once, when Roy was about five he walked in the kitchen and saw his father attempting to kill his mother. It was a terrible scene and Roy was there to watch it all."
>
> The tremor was instant. All my perceptions, all my judgment shattered, and I saw past the facade in the reality. I saw past the obnoxious adult to the traumatized little boy that I wanted to take in my arms and

comfort. I never looked at Roy the same again. I knew his secret, or of his secrets, and I understood.[30]

Having spent a lifetime learning how to interpret what we see and hear, we now are invited to turn off the interpretation. Instead of re-writing others' stories with our interpretations, we listen carefully to hear their stories, their hearts, their hopes. This isn't easy.

I think this is sage counsel: "Resolve to be tender with the young, compassionate with the aged, sympathetic with the striving and tolerant of the weak and the strong. Sometime in life you will have been all of these."[31]

Reflection:

Think of a time when you have listened carefully to what one of your children is telling you with his or her words and actions.

How did it feel? _____

_____

_____

What helped you get there? _____

_____

_____

How can you get there again? _____

_____

_____

How can you make that experience more common for you?_____

_____

_____

---

30 Carol Lynn Pearson, "Secrets," *New Era*, March 1984, 17.
31 "Quotes by Bob Goddard," http://www.zaadz.com/quotes/Bob_Goddard/.

Applying this strategy:

☐ I ask Father for help.

☐ I remember (with gratitude) past successes with this strategy.

☐ I ask myself, does this strategy fit me? If not, can I adapt it or should I discard it?

☐ I plan my response for next time the challenge arises.

☐ I imagine or pre-experience the better way of responding.

☐ I try it out.

☐ I keep refining my efforts—otherwise known as repenting.

Notes on my progress: _____

_____

_____

_____

_____

_____

_____

15. Be on the same team.

Humans tend to divide the human race up into teams—often just two teams: Us and Them. There are those we know and like. There are those we mistrust and may dislike.

There actually is a systematic bias in the way we see people. Humans tend to blame their own mistakes on their circumstances. "I was under a lot of pressure!" Meanwhile we tend to blame other people's mistakes on their lack of character. "He's not very honest." "She's lazy." Maybe this bias is a result of the fact that we know more about the pressures we face than we know about the pressures that others face.

So, I'm one of the good guys and you're a bad guy. You can imagine the mischief this causes when we divide up *within* families. Maybe I have a hard time with one of the children and I tend to see laziness, meanness, dishonesty, and selfishness in that child. In many cases, that child is much like all other children. In some way, that child bothers me—maybe because he or she reminds me of my own weaknesses. But if I start looking for badness, I will surely find it!

We may not realize how much this way of seeing a person is a choice. We choose to be irritated with something our children do. We choose to wonder about their character. We choose to start looking for more evidence of their badness. We feel justified in our judgment by the new evidence we find.

Irving Becker wisely identified how this bias affects our attitudes toward people: "If you don't like someone, the way he holds his spoon will make you furious; if you do like him, he can turn his plate over into your lap and you won't mind."[32]

---

32 *Reader's Digest Pocket Treasury of Great Quotations* (Pleasantville, N.Y: Reader's Digest, 1975), xx.

So we can choose to be painfully mortal—chafing over this discontent or that and organizing our complaints—or we can choose to be like Jesus—looking with compassion, striving to help, acknowledging our own humanness.

In Stephen Robinson's parable of the bicycle, he points out that we are all woefully short of the needed cash to buy the yearned-for bike. "When the cost of the bicycle is over one hundred dollars, what possible difference can it make in the long run that I lacked one hundred but you lacked only ninety-nine? We are both beggars at the mercy of God. Therefore, I can feel no superiority over the least struggling member. I can only feel empathy for someone who shares my own situation."[33]

Rather than letting differences in preference or style become a source of irritation and judgment, we can make creative use of our differences. For example, rather than reacting to our children's music as if it were the mayhem of a train wreck, we can invite them to teach us about the group, the lyrics, and what they enjoy about it. Or, at least, we can ask them to close the door when they play their stereo.

Instead of seeing the children as aliens sent to torment us, we see them as family members, fellow travelers in the mortal journey, brothers and sisters. We offer healing kindness and compassion. That is what being on the same team is all about.

Reflection:

Think of a time when you have encouraged the sense of being on the same team with your children.

---

33 Stephen E. Robinson, *Believing Christ* (Salt Lake City: Deseret Book, 1992), 51–52.

How did it feel? _____

_____

What helped you get there? _____

_____

How can you get there again? _____

_____

How can you make that experience more common for you? _____
·

_____

Applying this strategy:

☐ I ask Father for help.

☐ I remember (with gratitude) past successes with this strategy.

☐ I ask myself, does this strategy fit me? If not, can I adapt it or should I discard it?

☐ I plan my response for next time the challenge arises.

☐ I imagine or pre-experience the better way of responding.

☐ I try it out.

☐ I keep refining my efforts—otherwise known as repenting.

Notes on my progress: _____

_____

_____

_____

_____

_____

16. Make sure your actions match your words.

Children only learn the meaning of our words by connecting them to our actions. When our words and actions don't match, they believe our actions and ignore our words.

For example, parents all over the world tell their children to put on their shoes or they will be left behind when the family goes to church. Then we scurry off to ready ourselves and our Sunday School lessons. We return a few minutes later and find that the child has played around in the interim. The shoes are not on the feet. We explode, "I told you to put on your shoes!"

Our children might reasonably respond (if they were able to express themselves in this way), "Actually you offered me options. I thought the stay-at-home option sounded pretty good. When you dashed off, I reasonably supposed that I was free to choose. I think I'll stay home and play."

Or they might say, "Based on experience, I only think you're serious about my shoes when you turn red and start to scream. Until then, I assume you are just talking for fun."

This lesson is vital for the soft-spoken parent. We often ask children to do things but we don't send clear messages. We leave them wondering if we mean it. When they don't do what we have asked, we become angry. We wonder, "Why don't they do what we ask?" But our children might ask, "Why do you so often ask me to do things when it is clear that you don't intend to follow up. I believe your actions more than your words."

See if any of these situations seem familiar:

"If you don't eat your dinner, you can't have dessert." They don't eat dinner and they still get dessert.

"I'm counting to three!" When we get to three, we issue a new threat. Finally we scream: "I don't know what I'm going to do with you!"

"Clean up your room or you can't go out to play." We get distracted. They go out and play while the room remains a wreck.

"You may not have a candy bar." We get tired of whining so we provide a candy bar.

Often when our children do not respond to our weak requests, we get mad at the children. Yet we share responsibility. We need to say only those things that we intend to enforce. We should make our actions match our words.

For example, when we ask children to put on shoes, we might help them get started. Or we might have an older sibling help them. Or we might take a few minutes to make a game of it with them. Or we might take the child and the shoes and get them together in the car.

My colleague Laura allowed her boys to watch cartoons only after they were fully dressed and ready for school. Our friend Toni had a rule that the children were not to bring cookies into the living room. When Toni's daughter Julie wandered into the living room bearing a cookie, Toni could invite: "Oh! You want a cookie. Let's go in the kitchen to eat it." Another parent, Susan, had an agreement with her daughter that she would practice the piano for thirty minutes before dinner. When the daughter forgot, the dinner was saved until the practicing was completed.

We should only make rules that are important enough to enforce. Some may protest, "But that takes so much time!" I'm guessing that a scientific study would find that parents who take time to be sure that their requests are taken seriously will invest hundreds of hours *less* time over a lifetime than the parents who nag, cajole, and concede. And they will have lower blood pressure and better relationships with their children.

An ounce of prevention is worth a ton of preaching.

Reflection:

Think of a time when you have made your actions match your words—and have done it in kind ways.

How did it feel? _____

_____

_____

What helped you get there? _____

_____

_____

How can you get there again? _____

_____

_____

How can you make that experience more common for you? _____

_____

_____

Applying this strategy:

☐ I ask Father for help.

☐ I remember (with gratitude) past successes with this strategy.

☐ I ask myself, does this strategy fit me? If not, can I adapt it or should I discard it?

☐ I plan my response for next time the challenge arises.

☐ I imagine or pre-experience the better way of responding.

Make sure your actions match your words.

☐ I try it out.
☐ I keep refining my efforts—otherwise known as repenting.

Notes on my progress: _____

_____

_____

_____

_____

_____

_____

17. Blame it on the rain.

A few years ago two dear friends called me from a distant city. Their voices betrayed their exhaustion. "We've had trouble with Breck lately. We don't know what to do. We're desperate. Will you help us?"

The weary parents described the stresses around their recent move to a new city. The dad's new job entailed long hours leaving very little time or energy for his family. The mom was overwhelmed with the demands of the move and organizing the household.

Six-year-old Breck had started acting angry and hostile. Every day he would battle against getting on the bus. He seemed almost to take joy in torturing his mother as she tried to rush him to the school bus that was holding up traffic by fighting with her. "It seems that he is deliberately trying to manipulate me," observed the frustrated mother. "I think he wants to use his power to control the family. He seems to enjoy it."

When the mother asked me if I believed that Breck was trying to manipulate her, my instinctive response was, "No. I know Breck. He is an earnest, sweet, normal boy whose worst fault may be that he is tender and a perfectionist. I think he is saying, 'I am so confused about this move! I like to have some order in my life, but I have been torn away from friends, our old house, familiar routines...and now my mom and dad don't even want to snuggle with me at night because they say I need to be grown up. I feel desperately confused and lonely! Please! Please! Someone help me!'"

Seeing Breck as a lonely, confused boy leads to a parenting response very different from the one that would result from seeing him as devious and contrary. Bringing him up in light and truth includes seeing him in the best possible light—as a little boy wanting to be good but feeling very lost, lonely, and overwhelmed.

Rather than accuse, confront, and threaten, parents might respond to the message of pain and confusion that the boy's behavior represents. They can help the troubled boy against their common enemies of confusion, alienation, and fear. His father might say, "Wow! Son, you are really angry. Shall we run around the block together so that you can show me your anger?" Or mother might say, "Son, this all seems so confusing. Can we snuggle together in the rocking chair?" There are probably many more ideas that are still better. And parents are uniquely qualified, based on experience and inspiration, to know what will work with a given child in a specific circumstance. There are many responses that might help the boy deal with his immediate anger and confusion.

Long term solutions to help the boy might include arranging for the mother to volunteer at school so that she could be with her boy during the difficult weeks of transition to a new school. Dad might carve out some time for his son on the weekends. Mom might have the boy stay home from school with her once a week to have time together for a picnic. The family might invite one of Breck's classmates over to play at the house after school to help him build new friendships.

When children cannot find a good way to get their needs met, they may resort to terrorism—not out of spiteful nastiness, but out of desperation. Maybe rather than wanting power over the family, Breck really wanted to feel a little power in his own life. Maybe rather than trying to manipulate and punish the family, he really wanted to feel loved and safe.[34]

---

34 Story adapted from H. W. Goddard's "Divine parenting: The atonement of Jesus Christ is the key," *My Soul Delighteth in the Scriptures: Personal and Family Applications.* ed. H. W. Goddard & R. H. Cracroft (Salt Lake City, UT: Bookcraft, 1999).

That's why I say to blame it on the rain. Think about the rain that is falling in your child's life. Think about the stresses in his or her life. Think about the stresses in the family that might make your child feel anxious or lonely. A move? Health problems? Stress? Money problems?

The bad behavior we see in children is often due to the thunderstorm in their lives. So, blame it on the rain rather than blame it on badness in the child.

Reflection:

Think of a time when you have recognized the circumstances that make it hard for your child to be peaceful and loving. Think of a time when you have tried to understand the pressures in your child's life.

How did it feel? _____

_____

_____

What helped you get there? _____

_____

_____

How can you get there again? _____

_____

_____

How can you make that experience more common for you?_____

_____

_____

Applying this strategy:

☐ I ask Father for help.

☐ I remember (with gratitude) past successes with this strategy.

☐ I ask myself, does this strategy fit me? If not, can I adapt it or should I discard it?

Blame it on the rain.

☐ I plan my response for next time the challenge arises.
☐ I imagine or pre-experience the better way of responding.
☐ I try it out.
☐ I keep refining my efforts—otherwise known as repenting.

Notes on my progress: _____

_____

_____

_____

_____

_____

_____

18. Argue with your own inner voice.

Since the natural man is an enemy to God—and to his children, it is not surprising that our natural inner voice is also uncivilized and unhelpful. Our first response to a problem is generally an accusation: "What were you thinking?" "What's wrong with you?" "Why don't you think?"

This is neither motivating nor informative. And the devil is its source. Actually, Satan is the great accuser. He is the one who thrives on mocking and minimizing us.

Jesus is our advocate (D&C 45:3–5). At the final judgment, he presents himself to the Father and lists his merits. He does not do this so that he can claim the best land down by the lake in Kolob. After making his claim on Heaven's goodness, he transfers it to us: "Wherefore, Father, spare these my brethren that believe on my name, that they may come unto me and have everlasting life" (D&C 45:5). What a friend we have in Jesus! What a blessing that we have an Advocate!

Contrast this with Shannon's experience. One evening her mother was expecting company and had been rushing around preparing last-minute details. Mother had snapped at Shannon because she hadn't done her homework or taken her bath. Mom lectured her about responsibility. Then, when Mom walked into the living room, she discovered that Shannon had been trying to help her mother by dusting and polishing the furniture. Mom realized her mistake and hugged her earnest little girl. But company was already arriving and Shannon's surprise was quickly forgotten.

Later that evening, after the company had departed, Mom tucked Shannon into bed. As she turned to leave, she noticed tears forming in Shannon's eyes. "What's the matter, Dear?" She asked. Shannon looked her mother in the eye and asked the question that weighed on her soul. "Mom, why is it that when I do something bad, we talk about it so much? But when I try to do something good, it seems like I'm the only one who remembers?"

Shannon's question challenges all parents. Why do we notice and discuss misdeeds so much while neglecting children's good intentions and best efforts?

Haim Ginott, the famous child psychologist, recommended that we be advocates for our children. That does not mean that we ignore all their problems and limitations. But it means that we look for the good in them. He said, "Nature always sides with the hidden flaw. [We] have the opposite role: to side with the hidden asset, to minimize children's deficiencies, intensify their experience, and enlarge their lives."[35]

So, when we are tempted to point the accusing finger at our children, we might choose instead to become their advocates. We remember their strengths. We might even see how their strengths cause some of the problems they deal with.

Wally's stubbornness is connected to his strong character.
Alan's temper may come from a tender heart that is easily injured.
Beth's whining may come from feeling left out when she likes to be included.

Of course if we have subdued our natural man and energized the man of Christ in our soul, we may trust our inner voice. We can trust the angels of our better nature.

---

35 Haim G. Ginott, *Teacher and Child* (New York: MacMillan, 1972), 179.

But any time we are filled with accusation, we would be wise to turn our backs on Old Scratch and follow the example of our Advocate. We use our talents to understand and appreciate our children.

Reflection:

Think of a time when you challenged the natural-man voice that dwells on the faults of your children. Think of a time when you have replaced accusation with appreciation.

How did it feel? _____

_____

_____

What helped you get there? _____

_____

_____

How can you get there again? _____

_____

_____

How can you make that experience more common for you?_____

_____

_____

Applying this strategy:

☐ I ask Father for help.

☐ I remember (with gratitude) past successes with this strategy.

☐ I ask myself, does this strategy fit me? If not, can I adapt it or should I discard it?

☐ I plan my response for next time the challenge arises.

☐ I imagine or pre-experience the better way of responding.

Argue with your own inner voice.

☐ I try it out.

☐ I keep refining my efforts—otherwise known as repenting.

Notes on my progress: _____

_____

_____

_____

_____

_____

_____

19. Imagine yourself watching a stage play.

It is easy to get swept up into the drama of our lives so that we can no longer see things as they really are. We become so engaged in playing our part that we see nothing and think about nothing but our own oft-rehearsed lines.

John Gottman's research on marriage has made an intriguing discovery that is related to the challenges of parenting. When couples are angry and insult each other, they may think they are being clever and creative. But Gottman's research shows that angry couples follow a tired, familiar path. He even describes the four stages in the conflict process.[36] In contrast, when couples are happy, it is impossible to predict what they will do next.

The keen irony is that Satan is not remotely creative. "And that wicked one cometh and *taketh away light and truth*" (D&C 93:39, emphasis added). He has developed an engaging but trite process for people to relate to each other. Conflict is his theme and it is dreary, predictable stuff.

In contrast, when we are under God's influence, we are genuinely creative. The Creator is ultimately original, imaginative, inventive, and ingenious! And he inspires creativity in those who seek his mind and will. The love, joy, and peace that uniquely come from him are filled with delight and surprise.

So, if we can extract ourselves from the part that Satan has written for us, we may get to a better place. One way to do this is to remove ourselves from the role of judge, corrector, and accuser. We may step out of our part and take a seat in the audience. From that vantage point we may be able to see that our day's stress is speaking more loudly than any discernment about the child's needs. We may be able to see a struggling and imperfect child confronted by a tired, irritated and imperfect parent. If we can extract

---

36 See John M. Gottman, *Why Marriages Succeed or Fail* (New York: Simon and Schuster, 1994).

ourselves from the thoughts and emotions, we may be able to write a new—and more creative—part for us to play. We may even find words and acts that God has written for us.

I remember sitting with a Shirley W., the principal at a school for children with disabilities. When a class bell rang and two boys came to her door, she excused herself from our conversation. One boy told her about the things he had accomplished. She warmly congratulated him. The second boy asked, "What about me?" She reflected. Then she exploded, "I heard what you did to the substitute teacher." She grabbed the little boy and pulled him close. "You're too good a person to act that way! If you ever do that again, I will hug you senseless."

I fought back tears. Shirley had risen above the usual rant and threats. She chose to step out of the familiar part. She chose instead to send a clear message of affection—with limits.

Once we have applied godly creativity to re-writing our parenting parts, we may re-enter the play. Maybe we decide that we will confront the Big Issue later—but right now, let's hug. Or let's cook dinner. Or let's go buy a pizza. You just never know what you will come up with when God is your playwright.

Reflection:

Think of a time when you have removed yourself from the automatic and unhelpful responses and have let God fill your heart.
How did it feel? _____

_____

_____

What helped you get there? _____

_____

How can you get there again? _____

_____

How can you make that experience more common for you?_____

_____

Applying this strategy:

☐ I ask Father for help.

☐ I remember (with gratitude) past successes with this strategy.

☐ I ask myself, does this strategy fit me? If not, can I adapt it or should I discard it?

☐ I plan my response for next time the challenge arises.

☐ I imagine or pre-experience the better way of responding.

☐ I try it out.

☐ I keep refining my efforts—otherwise known as repenting.

Notes on my progress: _____

_____

_____

_____

_____

_____

20. Go walking.

Research has shown that mild exercise—such as walking—may be the most reliable way to lift our moods.

President McKay suggested walking as a solution for heated tempers between a man and his wife: "When you get into a discussion, only one get angry at a time.... You go outside and walk around the block, and then when you get back home, throw your hat in the door. If it comes back out again, walk around the block another time."[37]

The same general principle applies in relationships with our children. When we are angry, we would do well to take a walk. As George Jean Nathan observed, "No man can think clearly when his fists are clenched." Taking a walk can clear our heads and unclench our mental fists.

The walk is likely to be helpful if we use the time to enjoy God's world. The time is likely to be unproductive if we mentally heap hot coals upon our children's heads.

So, when we're feeling angry or irritable, we might take a walk. We can enjoy Mother Nature. We might even reflect on the mistakes *we* made that irritated *our* parents. There are also times when we might take the offending child with us—not to lecture or threaten—but to relax. As our focus turns from our irritation to our blessings, we are likely to have a more helpful perspective.

---

37 As quoted by Vaughn J. Featherstone in "The Torchbearer," *Speeches,* 5 June 1983, Brigham Young University, http://speeches.byu.edu/reader/reader.php?id=6871

Reflection:

Think of a time when you have taken a walk to calm yourself.
How did it feel? _____

_____

_____

What helped you get there? _____

_____

_____

How can you get there again? _____

_____

_____

How can you make that experience more common for you? _____

_____

_____

Applying this strategy:

☐ I ask Father for help.

☐ I remember (with gratitude) past successes with this strategy.

☐ I ask myself, does this strategy fit me? If not, can I adapt it or should I discard it?

☐ I plan my response for next time the challenge arises.

☐ I imagine or pre-experience the better way of responding.

☐ I try it out.

☐ I keep refining my efforts—otherwise known as repenting.

Notes on my progress: _____

_____

_____

_____

21. Think redemptively. ✦

I once read a story about an older woman who went to the grocery store and bought just a few items almost every day. The clerks wondered about this. Why didn't she buy groceries for a week? Why did she come in every day and buy just a few items? They couldn't figure out the answer, so one of the clerks determined to ask the woman. The next day, when the lady was ready to check out, the clerk asked, "Ma'am, why is it that you shop every day and buy just a few items?" The woman sighed, "I'm a widow. I live with my nephew—and I hate his guts. When I die, I don't intend to leave him any groceries!"

That is a good example of small-minded thinking. We keep score and we make sure that we don't bless anyone we don't like. Notice that this mind-set puts us in a role only God should play. We decide each person's merit and we decide their reward.

But we're not very good Gods. God knows everything and loves perfectly. We do not. So we do a very poor job of playing God.

"For God sent *not* his Son into the world to condemn the world; but that the world through him might be saved" (John 3:17, emphasis added). He came to rescue us. His whole purpose is redemptive. It appears that he only allows us to suffer as much as is necessary to teach and purify us.

Some of us have more faith in suffering than he does. We assume that making children suffer will help them learn. In my view, that is dangerous thinking. God begs, even commands, us humans to stay out of the judging and punishing business (Mormon 8:20). He commands us to love one another as he has loved us.

He loves us redemptively. He suffered all things in order to rescue us. We want our children to learn the lessons of life. And the message of experience and research is clear: People learn best when they feel loved.

I love the story of a sweet six-year-old girl named Marcie who was confined to the hospital for a serious lung disorder. During her hospital stay, one of her baby teeth fell out. She put it under the pillow hoping that the tooth fairy could find her at the hospital. The night nurse was assigned to take the tooth and slip a dollar bill under her pillow. Because she loved little Marcie so much, she determined to put two dollars under her pillow when she took the tooth.

But it wasn't easy to find the chance to get the tooth. In the course of the evening there were various therapists, aides, and nurses. But finally she found the right moment and slipped the money under the pillow.

The next morning the head nurse asked how it went. The nurse observed that it had been a busy evening but she had done her job. The head nurse replied: "It must have been busy. This morning there was $12 under her pillow!"

That is grace! While I'm not sure that $12 is a reasonable price for a baby tooth, I applaud the spirit of graciousness that motivated the generosity.

God recommends that we exercise influence "by persuasion, by long-suffering, by gentleness and meekness, and by love unfeigned" (D&C 121:41). We should think redemptively!

Reflection:

Think of a time when you have thought about a child redemptively— wanting to bless, teach and rescue him or her.

How did it feel? _____

_____

What helped you get there? _____

_____

How can you get there again? _____

_____

How can you make that experience more common for you? ____

_____

_____

Applying this strategy:

☐ I ask Father for help.

☐ I remember (with gratitude) past successes with this strategy.

☐ I ask myself, does this strategy fit me? If not, can I adapt it or should I discard it?

☐ I plan my response for next time the challenge arises.

☐ I imagine or pre-experience the better way of responding.

☐ I try it out.

☐ I keep refining my efforts—otherwise known as repenting.

Notes on my progress: _____

_____

_____

_____

_____

_____

_____

22. Invite a debate.

A dear friend called me very agitated one day and asked to see me. We met. She told me that she had discovered that her husband had been stealing from his employer. She was furious. She intended to leave him.

We talked. We discussed learning and weaknesses and patience. After about an hour she was resolved to return to her marriage and try to help her husband. As we parted, I asked her, "Why did you come to me when you knew I would not encourage you to divorce?" She replied immediately, "That is why I came to you! I needed someone who could help me find a way to stay. I knew you would do that."

I applaud her integrity. Even though she wanted to leave a painful relationship, she sought counsel that would challenge her to stay.

We can do the same. When we are determined to act in ways that are lower than our highest standards, we can seek counsel from those we know will pull us up to our full stature. Who do you know whose love of goodness is so great that they will challenge your less noble actions?

In an ideal family, our spouses do this for us often. When the fire in our souls is pushing us to act harshly, a faithful spouse can invite us to set aside the rage in favor of reason. In fact, we may work with our spouse at peaceful times to develop a signal for just such emergencies. When Nancy sees my temperature rise above the rational range, she might invite, "I know you've been wanting to mow the lawn out back. Why don't you do that and then we can talk about the children later this evening."

In some cases we may be able to find that nobler voice in our own souls. We may be able to challenge our own less-than-noble impulses.

My wise father used to say that many decisions are hard because we are trying to justify an action that is less than our highest standard. Another way to identify a bad decision is to notice when we are trying way too hard to convince ourselves. The way Shakespeare described this condition is: "The lady doth protest too much, methinks."[38] Rather than strut and moralize to justify thoughts and actions that we know to be less than they ought, we can repent. And when we need help to do it, we can invite those who are friends of Heaven to challenge us.

Reflection:

Think of a time when you have invited a debate—when you have challenged your less noble thoughts with input from a spouse, friends, the Spirit, or your own soul.

How did it feel? _____

_____

_____

What helped you get there? _____

_____

_____

How can you get there again? _____

_____

_____

How can you make that experience more common for you?_____

_____

_____

---

38 William Shakespeare, *Hamlet*, III, ii, 239.

Applying this strategy:

☐ I ask Father for help.

☐ I remember (with gratitude) past successes with this strategy.

☐ I ask myself, does this strategy fit me? If not, can I adapt it or should I discard it?

☐ I plan my response for next time the challenge arises.

☐ I imagine or pre-experience the better way of responding.

☐ I try it out.

☐ I keep refining my efforts—otherwise known as repenting.

Notes on my progress: _____

_____

_____

_____

_____

_____

_____

23. Feed your spirit.

"Out of the abundance of the heart, the mouth speaketh" (Matthew 12:34). A parched, arid heart cannot sustain life or goodness.

There are many ways to feed our spirits. But there is a trick to doing it right. Many of us try to feed our spirits in the way that works for Brother Smith or Sister Jones. Or we try to do the things we have heard are guaranteed spirit builders. But, when we tramp along the road of obligation as if we were on a death march, our spirits do not get fed. In other words, each of us must find the way that best feeds our own spirits.

For example, my spirit soars when I write or teach about our remarkable Redeemer. I love it! But, in days-gone-by when I used to force myself to march lockstep through a book of scripture, my spirit sank, my soul squirmed.

Some people experience quiet meditation as the best way to find truth. Not me. I like to rummage through my files of stories about goodness, truth, and Jesus. I love to read an insightful book. I rejoice to have a conversation with Greg, James, or Andy. I enjoy writing about eternal truth.

And, in God's good grace, there are a multitude of other ways I feed my spirit that have nothing to do with "religion." I love painting a tired old room in our house. I enjoy re-arranging furniture. I am keen on woodworking. It seems that God is delighted to give us joy.

Heber C. Kimball made a delightful observation about God: "I am perfectly satisfied that my Father and my God is a cheerful, pleasant, lively, and good-natured Being. Why? Because I am cheerful, pleasant, lively, and good-natured when I have his Spirit. That is one reason why I know; and another is—the Lord said, through Joseph Smith, 'I delight in a glad heart and a cheerful countenance.' That arises from the perfection of his attributes; he is a jovial, lively person, and a beautiful man."[39] We almost certainly underestimate how much happiness God has available for us.

The best research on happiness[40] (in my opinion) suggests that there are three ways to increase our well-being. We can savor or appreciate the blessings in our lives. We can use our God-given gifts. And we can serve. Those are the three processes for growing our happiness.

So we cultivate a grateful heart, we make room in our lives for our hobbies, and we find ways to make the world a better place. Those are all good ways to feed our spirit.

Reflection:

Think of a time when you have fed your spirit—when you have done things that brought you joy, growth, and satisfaction.

How did it feel? _____

_____

_____

What helped you get there? _____

_____

_____

How can you get there again? _____

_____

_____

How can you make that experience more common for you?_____

_____

_____

---

39 Brigham Young, *Journal of Discourses,* November 6, 1864, Vol. 4, 222.
40 See Martin E. P. Seligman, *Authentic Happiness* (New York: Free Press, 2002). This book is not only an excellent summary of the research on happiness, it is also one of the best psychology books written in a decade.

Applying this strategy:

☐ I ask Father for help.

☐ I remember (with gratitude) past successes with this strategy.

☐ I ask myself, does this strategy fit me? If not, can I adapt it or should I discard it?

☐ I plan my response for next time the challenge arises.

☐ I imagine or pre-experience the better way of responding.

☐ I try it out.

☐ I keep refining my efforts—otherwise known as repenting.

Notes on my progress: _____

_____

_____

_____

_____

_____

_____

24. Put it into perspective.

Just as I was finishing graduate school, Nancy and I bought an almost-new car. It was quite a contrast with our old station wagon with fake-wood siding that was peeling off. Our children felt that the days of their humiliation might finally be over.

I remember the first time I drove the car off the lot after signing the papers. As I sat in the driver's seat enjoying the many things that worked properly, I noticed a small dent in the hood. Perhaps a mechanic had bent over the car and dented the hood with a tire gauge in his shirt pocket. It was a small dent. But for several months it was the only thing I saw when I looked at the car. I hardly noticed the shiny paint, the uncracked upholstery, or the hardy engine. I only saw the dent.

Most of us do the same thing in family life. We notice the little thing that isn't quite right. Sometimes it is the only thing we notice.

My son Andy has always been creative. As he got older he got more and more artistic. He has always been a kind, generous, and respectful boy. But, when he was a teenager, his creativity was more evident in his room than was his respect for the family rule about keeping his room clean.

We would remind him, but the creative projects would still accumulate. We would "consequence" him and leave his unhampered laundry unwashed. But he just didn't worry about tidiness the way his perfectionistic dad did.

We had two choices. We could increase the volume on the demand. Or we could let it go. We chose to let it go. We did not want to torch a relationship with our son for the sake of a little tidiness. (We did reserve the right to close his door when the disarray bothered us. And, once in a while, we asked if he would humor us by tidying things. He did so gladly.)

Many of the power struggles between parents and children are about matters of taste and preference. A mother may not like her daughter wearing T-shirts to school. It may suggest disrespect and rebellion to the mom. To the daughter it is merely a matter of personal expression.

If we over-interpret children's behavior as signifying rebellion, we are likely to over-react and create rebellion. As Chieko Okazaki advises, "In principles, great clarity. In practices, great charity."[41]

In contrast, if a child is wanting to buy a prom dress that is clearly immodest, we can empathize with her desire while setting a firm limit: "I can see why you like the dress. The fabric is elegant. We don't buy strapless gowns. Have you seen others that you like or do we need to keep looking?"

We can deliver a firm message without ever becoming disagreeable. When our daughter cries in desperation, "Mom! It's not that bad. It is exactly the dress I want. And Becky has one just like it. Don't be such a prude!" We can keep our balance. "Wow. You really like that dress! And I can see why. Since it is strapless, we can look at some other store or we might look online. Which sounds good to you?"

If we believe that we must convince our children that we are right and if we expect them to appreciate us in every moment, we will be disappointed. Good parenting requires us to set some limits that children will dislike. But we can always be pleasant.

And we can recognize that a lot of little choices should be left to them.

---

41 Chieko N. Okazaki, *Lighten Up* (Salt Lake City: Deseret Book, 1993), 17.

Reflection:

Think of a time when you have put children's actions in perspective—overlooking little mistakes and allowing them to follow their preferences. How did it feel?

_____

_____

What helped you get there? _____

_____

_____

How can you get there again? _____

_____

_____

How can you make that experience more common for you?_____

_____

_____

Applying this strategy:

☐ I ask Father for help.

☐ I remember (with gratitude) past successes with this strategy.

☐ I ask myself, does this strategy fit me? If not, can I adapt it or should I discard it?

☐ I plan my response for next time the challenge arises.

☐ I imagine or pre-experience the better way of responding.

☐ I try it out.

☐ I keep refining my efforts—otherwise known as repenting.

Notes on my progress: _____

_____

_____

25. Invite each child to be part of a solution.

God commands that we not allow our children to fight and quarrel with each other (Mosiah 4:14). He doesn't specify just how that is to be done. But I feel pretty sure that God doesn't want parents to break up sibling conflict by wading into the middle of the battle with bigger guns.

In my youth, I often picked fights with my brother Alan, who is a good-hearted, compassionate, good-natured guy. I myself have never had any real preference for unkindness or violence. But we still teased each other endlessly. I resolved disputes by locking Alan in a hall closet as long as I was bigger than he. Later I turned to goading and tormenting him verbally.

Mom and Dad tried everything they could think of to help us settle differences and to encourage peace.

On one occasion after I had been tormenting Alan, and when all efforts at negotiation and calm persuasion had failed, Dad suggested we wrestle. Well, Alan whipped me, which, incidentally, did not bring peace and understanding to our relationship; my determination to conquer only increased. On another occasion Mom and Dad suggested that we settle our differences through a foot race. I outdistanced Alan. I am certain that his bond with me was not strengthened by being beaten in a race.

These methods of resolving differences did not bring peace and understanding—though they may have marginally increased our physical fitness. In fact, one strategy for dealing with bickering might be to direct children's anger toward physical contests and hope that maturity would set in to quell the rivalries. Such a decades-long process may have some advantages, yet it cannot teach skills of peacemaking.

I remember another occasion when Alan and I had been arguing over some small difference. Dad, a peace-loving man if ever there was one, was weary of the contention. He turned both of us to face him and invited each of us to tell our side of the story. Alan, through tears, told of my picking on him and rude treatment of him. When it was my turn, I calmly and sensibly told of Alan's misdeeds and carefully wove psychological explanation into the tale. As I told my story I warmed to the challenge and embellished the story with plausible though invented details. I knew that my Father was a very rational man. Alan was more likely to be judged in error by Dad. The only thing that process revealed was that I had a greater talent for creative story telling than Alan. Or, to be fair, I was better at lying than Alan who is, to this day, a very fine story teller.

There were times when Mom held the warring factions to an accounting. Mother, always sensitive to the underdog and emotional suffering, was more likely to see my error.

The irony in the investigation process is that every party in a war contributes something to the misunderstanding. While one party may contribute far more than another, it is impossible for any of us mortals to weigh guilt objectively and dispassionately. We all have biases.

My battles with Alan and the accounting before our parents underscore what may be the first law of human dynamics: When someone tries to take something away from us, we cling to it more tenaciously. If Dad or Mom tried to convince me that I was wrong, I would renew my data collecting and analyzing to prove I was right. I would also add passion and indignation. Given that the human tendency to see ourselves as right is almost universal, what's a parent (or any other negotiator) to do? How can we move people from the natural-man tendency to stake out a territory and defend it at all costs? How can we keep people from exaggerating their differences? How can we teach cooperation and harmony? How can we hope to establish peace in our families?

I have an idea. Imagine that Dad had very attentively listened to the two separate dramas as if they did not have to be woven into one story. He could listen for each person's personal reality. He might have said to Alan, "Son, it sounds as if you are tired of being pushed around. It sounds like you would like to be able to play in your bedroom without your brother telling you to get lost. Is that right?" Alan, through words and gestures, will tell Dad whether he has captured the emotional essence of his experience.

Then Dad might turn to me. "Wally, it sounds as if you would like to be able to work on your projects without being interrupted. You would like your brother not to bother you when you are in the middle of something. Is that right?" As Dad attempts to understand each of our perspectives, he is inviting our cooperation and trust.

When each of us feels understood, we are prepared to offer compassion. We are ready to look for solutions. "I wonder if you boys have any ideas how you can solve those problems?" In such a setting I might have volunteered, "Well, I could be nicer to Alan. And I could let him know when I really need quiet."

At Dad's invitation Alan might have volunteered to be more quiet when he could see that I was concentrating. He might also have volunteered to play outside when I was working on some projects.

When people are looking for solutions rather than problems, wonderful things can happen. When their better natures have been invoked, people may choose to offer kindness and sacrifice for the common good.

By the way, I cannot imagine that anyone on the face of the earth had better parents than Alan, Beth, Brent, Paul, Bryan, Lorene, Levi, and me. But no one ever taught our folks how to draw solutions out of us kids.

Reflection:

Think of a time when you have invited your children to be part of the solution in their disagreements with their siblings.

How did it feel? _____

_____

_____

What helped you get there? _____

_____

_____

How can you get there again? _____

_____

_____

How can you make that experience more common for you?_____

_____

_____

Applying this strategy:

- ☐ I ask Father for help.
- ☐ I remember (with gratitude) past successes with this strategy.
- ☐ I ask myself, does this strategy fit me? If not, can I adapt it or should I discard it?
- ☐ I plan my response for next time the challenge arises.
- ☐ I imagine or pre-experience the better way of responding.
- ☐ I try it out.
- ☐ I keep refining my efforts—otherwise known as repenting.

Invite each child to be part of a solution.

Notes on my progress: _____

_____

_____

_____

_____

_____

_____

26. Choose to see the good.

I remember a story about a Little League coach who had players who just didn't get baseball. They rarely hit the ball and couldn't seem to remember which way to run the bases. Naturally, they didn't win many games. In fact, they lost every game of the season.

Then came the last game of the season. In the last inning of that last game, the coach's team was only down by one run. As fate would have it, the next person up to bat was a little boy who had never hit the ball or caught it in the entire season. Since there were two outs against the team already, the team was ready to bag the bats and balls ending the season without a single win.

But somehow that little boy connected with the pitch. After some pause for amazement, he made his way to first base. At this point the guys realized that the next batter was their best. Hopes rose. The team might end the season with a win!

The ball was pitched. The slugger hit it squarely toward right field! With a little coaching, the feckless boy on first headed toward second base. But he hadn't gone very far before he saw the ball coming toward him. He had never been in this situation. He wasn't sure what to do.

So he caught the ball making the final out. The coach's team lost the game and the season.

The coach must have been shocked. He thought for a moment and then turned to his stunned team. "Cheer for that boy! He has never before hit the ball or caught it and he just did both in the same inning!"

The boy's parents later thanked the coach. That little boy had never even been played in a game before that season. Now he was a local hero.

That coach saw good where others might have seen failure. He saw progress.

Research[42] shows a clear way of discouraging ourselves and others. When anyone makes a mistake, we can make it personal, permanent, and pervasive (the 3 P's). To the child who forgets to feed the dog, the discouraging statement might be: "How could you be so careless?! What's wrong with you?" (personal), "It seems like you never remember anything!" (permanent), "You forget your homework, you forget to take your scriptures to church," "I think you would forget your head if it weren't screwed on" (pervasive).

While the parent may intend to motivate more reliable remembering, the child will almost surely experience discouragement. In contrast, a parent might choose to see the good. "You usually remember to feed the dog. You must have a lot on your mind."

By making the problem situational, temporary, and limited, the child is more likely to see it as solvable. In fact, a parent might ask, "What could you do to help yourself remember to feed the dog? Would it help to put a reminder on your closet door?"

Of course choosing to see the good is not limited to seeing good in bad situations. We should notice and appreciate the many small ways children try to be helpful. "Thank you for helping your brother." "Thank you for helping me clear the table." "Thank you for that big hug. You made my day!"

Reflection:

Think of a time when you have chosen to see the good in a child—when you could have ignored the behavior or could have been negative but instead chose to see the good.

---

42 See Martin Seligman's *Learned Optimism* (New York: Free Press, 1998).

How did it feel? _____

_____

What helped you get there? _____

_____

How can you get there again? _____

_____

How can you make that experience more common for you? _____

_____

_____

Applying this strategy:

☐ I ask Father for help.

☐ I remember (with gratitude) past successes with this strategy.

☐ I ask myself, does this strategy fit me? If not, can I adapt it or should I discard it?

☐ I plan my response for next time the challenge arises.

☐ I imagine or pre-experience the better way of responding.

☐ I try it out.

☐ I keep refining my efforts—otherwise known as repenting.

Notes on my progress: _____

_____

_____

_____

_____

_____

27. Invite the child to talk you out of it.

As children get older they should be more and more involved in guiding their own lives. There may be times when we are inclined to be angry with a child or impose a stern penalty, but we are not sure what will help them. Maybe we could ask them. We can invite children to tell us what would help them remember their chores, get ready for school, or be helpful with a sibling.

When we are inclined to impose a stiff penalty designed more by anger than reason, we can instead invite the child to help us find the right consequence. "After what you said to your sister, I'm tempted to remove all your privileges for decades. I'm really upset. I need you to tell me what would help you take this seriously."

The children usually know better than we do the things that will help the messages sink in for them.

Reflection:

Think of a time when you have let a child help you design the consequence for his or her misdeeds.

How did it feel? _____

_____

_____

What helped you get there? _____

_____

_____

How can you get there again? _____

_____

_____

How can you make that experience more common for you?_____

_____

_____

Applying this strategy:

☐ I ask Father for help.

☐ I remember (with gratitude) past successes with this strategy.

☐ I ask myself, does this strategy fit me? If not, can I adapt it or should I discard it?

☐ I plan my response for next time the challenge arises.

☐ I imagine or pre-experience the better way of responding.

☐ I try it out.

☐ I keep refining my efforts—otherwise known as repenting.

Notes on my progress: _____

_____

_____

_____

_____

_____

_____

28. Have charity.

Arthur Bowler wrote about a minister and his cherished hymnal. One day the minister's two-year-old got a hold of the book and applied a pen to making scribbles all over the first page. When his father walked into the room, the little boy cowered. The father, a man who cherished his books, walked to the boy picked up the hymnal, studied it carefully, and sat down without a word. The little boy awaited his punishment. But rather than punish or scold, the father took the pen from the boy's hand and wrote alongside the scribbles: "John's word 1959, age two."

When we let love rule in our hearts, our reactions are very different from those when Satan rules. This father chose to see the book sanctified and blessed by the scribbles of his cherished boy.

Van Wyck Brooks has written, "How delightful is the company of generous people, who overlook trifles and keep their minds instinctively fixed on whatever is good and positive in the world about them. People of small caliber are always carping. They are bent on showing their own superiority, their knowledge or prowess or good breeding. But magnanimous people have no vanity, they have no jealousy, and they feed on the true and the solid wherever they find it. And, what is more, they find it everywhere."[43]

Of course there is a very specific kind of love that motivates such graciousness. We call it charity—the pure love of Christ. It causes us to love as he loves. Charity changes everything. It warms our perceptions and sweetens our reactions. It does not mean that all demands disappear. It means that our actions are guided with one purpose in mind: blessing another person.

---

43 Van Wyck Brooks, *A Chillmark Miscellany: Essays Old and New* (New York: Octagon Books, 1973).

How do we get this divine blessing of charity? Mormon's answer is simple and direct:

> Wherefore, my beloved brethren, *pray unto the Father with all the energy of heart*, that ye may be filled with this love, which he hath bestowed upon all who are true followers of his Son, Jesus Christ; that ye may become the sons of God; that when he shall appear we shall be like him, for we shall see him as he is; that we may have this hope; that we may be purified even as he is pure. (Moroni 7:47–48, emphasis added)

It is not casual prayer but whole-hearted pleading that yields this reward. When charity comes, it is more than a fleeting feeling; it is the culmination of our efforts to fill ourselves with Christ. It includes all our efforts to honor sacred relationships while seeking divine influence.

A story about William Faulkner captures this attitude. The great author made an informal presentation at the University of Mississippi. The student assigned to guide him had been anxious about interacting with a man of genius and fame but found that he was completely approachable and down-to-earth.

Faulkner had spent more than two hours with the students and faculty when his guide noticed him checking his watch. The guide wondered if he had an important commitment and asked him if he needed to leave. He replied: "Well, it's just that I promised my daughter Jill that I'd help her shell corn for the chickens and I don't want to disappoint her."

Charity can take the simple form of a willingness to honor our commitments to our children.

Reflection:

Think of a time when you have shown charity to one of your children.
How did it feel? _____

_____

_____

What helped you get there? _____

_____

_____

How can you get there again? _____

_____

_____

How can you make that experience more common for you?_____

_____

_____

Applying this strategy:

☐ I ask Father for help.

☐ I remember (with gratitude) past successes with this strategy.

☐ I ask myself, does this strategy fit me? If not, can I adapt it or should I
  discard it?

☐ I plan my response for next time the challenge arises.

☐ I imagine or pre-experience the better way of responding.

☐ I try it out.

☐ I keep refining my efforts—otherwise known as repenting.

Notes on my progress: _____

_____

_____

_____

_____

29. Imagine yourself as Aunt Mary.

Aunt Mary and Uncle Grant lived in Blanding, Utah. Every summer they invited us to come visit them. I wonder why. We added to their burdens—yet they seemed to genuinely enjoy us. And they tolerated our antics without visible chagrin. When I crashed his motor scooter with no injury to me but no benefit for the scooter, Uncle Grant merely laughed. When Alan and I narrowly avoided burning down all of southern Utah, Aunt Mary simply turned on the sprinklers to cool us off as we dragged back to her house.

There is something magical about a person who seems to genuinely enjoy you in spite of foibles and misdeeds. I'm grateful for Aunt Mary and Uncle Grant.

Maybe you know someone who has always seen the best in you. Maybe your life has been blessed by that person's generosity. Think back to the sweet blessing of that heavenly gift. Savor it. Re-live specific episodes.

Now, are we ready to be Aunt Marys for our children? Are we ready to look beyond their goofiness and see their spunk? Are we willing to be inconvenienced by the demands of parenting? Are we willing to bring surprise and joy to our relationship?

When we fill our souls with remembered goodness, we are better prepared to offer grace to those we love. We can offer a special picnic, a trip to the zoo, an outing in the backyard. And we can savor every moment.

Reflection:

Think of a time when you have been an Aunt Mary for one of your children.

How did it feel? _____

_____

_____

What helped you get there? _____

_____

_____

How can you get there again? _____

_____

_____

How can you make that experience more common for you? ___

_____

_____

Applying this strategy:

☐ I ask Father for help.

☐ I remember (with gratitude) past successes with this strategy.

☐ I ask myself, does this strategy fit me? If not, can I adapt it or should I discard it?

☐ I plan my response for next time the challenge arises.

☐ I imagine or pre-experience the better way of responding.

☐ I try it out.

☐ I keep refining my efforts—otherwise known as repenting.

Notes on my progress: _____

_____

_____

_____

_____

_____

_____

30. Pray for mercy.

The standard prayer sounds pretty much like dickering at a swap meet. "I was just wondering if I could trade you all my work and suffering for some of the goodies I want. Let's make a deal."

The problem is that God doesn't owe us anything. We are deeply in his debt while he owes us nothing. What he gives to us, he gives out of love, not obligation. Our efforts to put him in our debt are futile—or worse, insulting.

The pattern of scripture is different from the approach we often instinctively take.

> Do not say: O God, I thank thee that we are better than our brethren; but rather say: *O Lord, forgive my unworthiness, and remember my brethren in mercy—yea, acknowledge your unworthiness before God at all times.* (Alma 38:14, emphasis added)

Praying for mercy is not only the action recommended by scripture, it is also the pattern followed by those who sought God successfully. Consider the prayer of the brother of Jared, the prayer that opened the veil for him.

> O Lord, thou hast said that we must be encompassed about by the floods. *Now behold, O Lord, and do not be angry with thy servant because of his weakness before thee; for we know that thou art holy and dwellest in the heavens, and that we are unworthy before thee; because of the fall our natures have become evil continually; nevertheless, O Lord, thou hast given us a commandment that we must call upon thee, that from thee we may receive according to our desires.*

Behold, O Lord, thou hast smitten us because of our iniquity, and hast driven us forth, and for these many years we have been in the wilderness; nevertheless, thou hast been merciful unto us. O Lord, look upon me in pity, and turn away thine anger from this thy people, and suffer not that they shall *go forth across this raging deep in darkness;* but behold these things which I have molten out of the rock.

And I know, O Lord, that *thou hast all power,* and can do whatsoever thou wilt for the benefit of man; therefore touch these stones, O Lord, with thy finger, and prepare them that they may shine forth in darkness; and they shall shine forth unto us in the vessels which we have prepared, that we may have light while we shall cross the sea. (Ether 3:2–4, emphasis added)

The most dramatic and effective of all scriptural prayers for mercy may be that uttered by Alma.

Now, as my mind caught hold upon this thought, I cried within my heart: *O Jesus, thou Son of God, have mercy on me,* who am in the gall of bitterness, and am encircled about by the everlasting chains of death. (Alma 36:18, emphasis added)

This prayer carried Alma from being among the vilest of sinners to a vision of God! The same prayer apparently has great power for groups as well. Consider the collective prayer of the people who had been taught by King Benjamin:

And they had viewed themselves in their own carnal state, even less than the dust of the earth. And they all cried aloud with one voice, saying: *O have mercy, and apply the atoning blood of Christ that we may receive forgiveness of our sins, and our hearts may be purified;* for we believe in Jesus Christ, the Son of God, who created heaven and

123

earth, and all things; who shall come down among the children of men. (Mosiah 4:2, emphasis added)

The call for mercy was recommended by Jesus in the old world. The man who was right with God was the one who threw himself on the merits, mercy, and grace of him who is mighty to save.

> And the publican, standing afar off, would not lift up so much as his eyes unto heaven, but smote upon his breast, saying, *God be merciful to me a sinner.*
>
> I tell you, this man went down to his house justified rather than the other: for every one that exalteth himself shall be abased; and he that humbleth himself shall be exalted. (Luke 18:13–14, emphasis added)

(For more scriptural examples of the "have mercy" pattern, see Mosiah 4:11, Psalms 6:2–4, Psalms 5:1, Isaiah 55:7, Psalms 57:1, Isaiah 54:8, 3 Nephi 22:8, Matthew 9:13, Matthew 12:7, Matthew 9:27–29, Matthew 15:22, Matthew 17:15, Matthew 20:30, Mark 10:47, Luke 18:47, Luke 17:12, 1 Nephi 8:8, 1 Nephi 21:13, Alma 2:29, Alma 3:14, Alma 12:33, Alma 15:8–11, Alma 18:40, Alma 19:29, Alma 34:17, Alma 38:7, Alma 38:14, 3 Nephi 9:14, Ether 12:27, D&C 106:7, D&C 109:34, 2 Nephi 9, Alma 26:21, Alma 7:23, Genesis 18:27–32, 2 Corinthians 12:10, Luke 15:16–22, Mormon 9:6, 2 Nephi 2:6–8, Alma 2:30, Alma 15:8–10, 1 Peter 5:5–6.)

Calling out for mercy is the cry of those who understand rightly their relationship with God.

We can apply this principle in our parenting. Rather than tell God how much he owes us for bearing with a child, we can go to him in humility: "Father, I come to Thee in humility. I don't deserve Thy help. We both know that I don't do as well as I should. I act impatiently and selfishly more than I can stand to confess. I come to Thee out of desperation. I simply cannot be the kind of parent my children need without Thy help. Wilt Thou grant me grace? Wilt Thou soften my heart and fill my mind? Wilt Thou give me charity?"

My testimony based on years of throwing myself on his mercy is that God responds to such prayers with an outpouring of goodness.

Reflection:

Think of a time when you have called on God for mercy.

How did it feel? _____

_____

_____

What helped you get to that point of humble submission? _____

_____

_____

How can you get there again? _____

_____

_____

How can you make that experience of Divine help more common for you?

_____

_____

Applying this strategy:

☐ I ask Father for help.
☐ I remember (with gratitude) past successes with this strategy.
☐ I ask myself, does this strategy fit me? If not, can I adapt it or should I discard it?
☐ I plan my response for next time the challenge arises.

☐ I imagine or pre-experience the better way of responding.

☐ I try it out.

☐ I keep refining my efforts—otherwise known as repenting.

Notes on my progress: _____

_____

_____

_____

_____

_____

_____

31. Get help. ✐

When we're overwhelmed, overloaded, and over-stressed, our children are likely to get a brittle, demanding parent. We may not realize how different we seem to our children. In fact, our pain can make us oblivious to their struggles and feelings.

Some dear friends wrote to us from a distant city asking for advice in helping their son. Once in a while he seemed to go crazy, running around the house and jumping on the furniture in defiance of family rules. Mom and Dad emailed me, asking what they could do.

I wrote back the standard advice about noticing the stress in the child's life, being sure he has loving time with mom and dad, and giving him many chances to use his energy and talents. When I didn't hear back from them for some time, I hoped things were going better.

Then we got another email asking for a chance to talk by phone. "We're so frustrated we fear that we will hurt our little boy." We set a time to talk.

At the appointed time, they called us. For more than an hour we talked about the boy's stresses, his loving opportunities with parents, and ways to use his energy. But we didn't find the answer to the episodes.

In desperation, I asked the mom, "Is there anything different from the usual in *your* life at the time of these episodes?"

Mom heaved a sigh. "Every once in a while I am up all night with the baby when he is sick. When morning comes, I am exhausted. Our problems almost always occur when I am sitting nursing the baby after being up all night."

I asked the logical follow-up question: "Is your boy pretty sensitive to your moods?"

Her immediate response: "He's very sensitive! He notices anytime anything is bothering me."

We had our answer. Every once in a while, the "terrorist" boy would get up and find that his normally-cheerful mother was distant and gloomy. He would feel worried, anxious, insecure. His behavior was his way of saying, "Mom, where are you? I need you! Please play with me! Please talk to me! Please be my mommy!" The little troublemaker was really just an anxious child who wanted his mama back.

Though it helps to understand the problem, there is no easy solution for it. Understanding the boy's anxiety, Mom might explain her exhaustion to him. She might also call a friend and ask if the son can play at their house while she takes a nap. Dad might take some time from work to care for the boys while his wife rests. They might call on a grandparent or a baby-sitter.

There are times when every parent needs a helping hand. That help may come from spouse, extended family, friend, or professional. When we are overloaded, we should get help.

Reflection:

Think of a time when you have been overloaded and have gotten help. How did it feel to draw in the needed resources? _____

_____

_____

What helped you get there? _____

_____

_____

Get help.

How can you get there again when appropriate? _____
_____
_____

Applying this strategy:

☐ I ask Father for help.

☐ I remember (with gratitude) past successes with this strategy.

☐ I ask myself, does this strategy fit me? If not, can I adapt it or should I discard it?

☐ I plan my response for next time the challenge arises.

☐ I imagine or pre-experience the better way of responding.

☐ I try it out.

☐ I keep refining my efforts—otherwise known as repenting.

Notes on my progress: _____
_____
_____
_____
_____
_____
_____

32. Remember your own mistakes.

Do you remember teasing your sister? Do you remember sneaking a candy bar from the pantry? Do you remember telling stories to cover your misdeeds? Do you remember using fireworks in ways that could have hurt someone?

All of us have been childish. All of us have made lots of mistakes.

Let's adapt a familiar parable.

> Therefore is the kingdom of heaven likened unto a certain grandfather, which would take account of his children.

> And when he had begun to reckon, one was brought unto him, which owed him a billion dollars.

> But forasmuch as he had not to pay, his grandfather commanded him to be sold, and his wife, and children, and all that he had, and payment to be made.

> The parent therefore fell down, and worshipped him, saying, Father, have patience with me, and I will pay thee all.

> Then the grandfather was moved with compassion, and loosed him, and forgave him the debt.

> But the same father went out, and found one of his children, which owed him ten bucks: and he laid hands on him, and took him by the throat, saying, Pay me that thou owest.

And his son fell down at his feet, and besought him, saying, Have patience with me, and I will pay thee all.

And he would not: but went and cast him into prison, till he should pay the debt.

So when other families in the neighborhood saw what was done, they were very sorry, and came and told unto the grandfather all that was done.

Then his grandfather, after that he had called him, said unto him, O thou wicked son, I forgave thee all that debt, because thou desiredst me:

Shouldest not thou also have had compassion on thy child, even as I had pity on thee?

And his father was wroth, and delivered him to the tormentors, till he should pay all that was due unto him.

So likewise shall my heavenly Father do also unto you, if ye from your hearts forgive not every one his children their trespasses. (Matthew 18:23–35, adapted)

Those of us who have such grievous debts on Heaven's account should show compassion to our own children as they struggle toward goodness.

Reflection:

Think of a time when you have remembered your own mistakes and shown compassion to a child.

How did it feel? _____

_____

_____

What helped you get there? _____

_____

_____

How can you get there again? _____

_____

_____

How can you make that experience more common for you?_____

_____

_____

Applying this strategy:

- ☐ I ask Father for help.
- ☐ I remember (with gratitude) past successes with this strategy.
- ☐ I ask myself, does this strategy fit me? If not, can I adapt it or should I discard it?
- ☐ I plan my response for next time the challenge arises.
- ☐ I imagine or pre-experience the better way of responding.
- ☐ I try it out.
- ☐ I keep refining my efforts—otherwise known as repenting.

Notes on my progress: _____

_____

_____

_____

_____

_____

33. Keep your eye on eternity.

Imagine that you own a modest farm in rural Wyoming.[44] You enjoy your work. You make just enough to get by. But one day everything is changed. You get a call from a powerful monarch. The king is inquiring whether you might allow the crown prince to come and work on the farm with you. "We want him to get some experience." You are speechless. "We don't expect you to change the way you live and work. Just be a good farmer and let him learn from you." You mutter a weak assent.

Thus it is with parenting. The heavenly King asks us to take a crown prince or princess into our home. At first we are unnerved by the responsibility. But as the weeks and months pass, the duties of the farm eclipse the awesome responsibility of mentoring royalty. In time our irritation over spilled milk and neglected chores exceeds our awe of office.

Viewing our parental responsibilities in an eternal perspective should change everything. Could I speak harshly and carelessly to my royal charge? Even after occasions of misbehavior, could I ever fail to see the nobility and potential in the growing child? Could I ever believe that a television program or magazine article was more important than a walk in the fields with the cherished guest? When his or her ideas are silly and childish, would I mock them? Or would I listen, understand, and counsel? In times of trouble would I shrug carelessly or would I beseech heaven with my whole soul in behalf of the errant child?

In the last few years we have added four princes and one princess to our family. Those cherished grandchildren, seen from the perspective of a man who has gained some experience since he raised his own children, are a heavenly gift. To hold them is an honor. To speak of them is a blessing.

---

44 Adapted from an article written for *Meridian Magazine* by author.

When our daughter called recently to tell us that their infant boy was ill and might require an operation, our hearts sank. As soon as the phone call was over we fell to our knees to plead for heavenly help. We would gladly give our lives to protect our cherished charges. God asks instead that we live our lives in loving and teaching them.

Maybe it is only in times of crisis that we fully recognize the blessing and responsibility of caring for the children of the divine King. In ways we don't fully understand we are eternally connected to each other and to him. Brigham Young taught, "Say your prayers always before going to work. Never forget that. A father—the head of the family—should never miss calling his family together and dedicating himself and them to the Lord of Hosts."[45]

An admired friend told about an experience with her 8-year-old daughter. The little girl wrote a song and sang it to her mother. The mother was amazed at the deep message. In her heart she asked: "Heavenly Father, who is this woman?" For a moment the veil parted and she saw her little girl as she really is: a magnificent woman, a glorious spiritual being! "I wanted to kneel at her feet." It changed the way she treated that child because she had seen her divine nature and heritage.

When the great King calls us Home, we will return with our dear children to his glorious presence. We will sit with him at that heavenly feast. And we will thank him that he entrusted us with some of his dearest children. Then will we all be Kings and Queens to the Most High God.

Reflection:

Think of a time when you have seen your children as cherished gifts from the King of Heaven.

---

45 *Discourses of Brigham Young*, ed. John A. Widtsoe (Salt Lake City: Deseret Book, 1954), 44.

How did it feel? _____

_____

What helped you get there? _____

_____

How can you get there again? _____

_____

How can you make that experience more common for you? _____

_____

_____

Applying this strategy:

☐ I ask Father for help.

☐ I remember (with gratitude) past successes with this strategy.

☐ I ask myself, does this strategy fit me? If not, can I adapt it or should I discard it?

☐ I plan my response for next time the challenge arises.

☐ I imagine or pre-experience the better way of responding.

☐ I try it out.

☐ I keep refining my efforts—otherwise known as repenting.

Notes on my progress: _____

_____

_____

_____

_____

_____

_____

34. Teach rather than preach. AA

Brigham Young taught that "parents should never drive their children, but lead them along, giving them knowledge as their minds are prepared to receive it. Chastening may be necessary betimes, but parents should govern their children by faith rather than by the rod, *leading them kindly by good example into all truth and holiness.*"[46]

Preaching has an impatient, condescending spirit to it. Teaching is different. It is about sharing and discovery. It honors the learner as an essential contributor.

Consider the importance of teaching social skills. Children who tend to get rejected at school are those who don't understand the rules of social interaction. A boy with that deficiency might try to enter a play group by grabbing a toy from one of his classmates. This does not endear him to the other children. He is scorned and rejected.

In contrast, popular children who want to join a play group are likely to stand at the periphery of play. When they see a way to help—maybe one of the children drops a toy—the popular child jumps to help. That person is welcomed into the circle of friendship.

How did the popular child learn this skill? Did a parent sit down and provide instruction on methods for entering play groups? Probably not. It is more likely that the popular child saw those methods used at home. The child may also have been taught how to welcome friends into their home, how to share with siblings, and how to deal with differences.

---

46 *Discourses of Brigham Young*, ed. John A. Widtsoe (Salt Lake City: Deseret Book, 1954), 208, emphasis added.

What a tragedy that so many children do not have anyone to teach them! In our roles as parents, neighbors, and teachers, I pray that we will reach out to the untrained children and help them find ways to be a part of our little communities of love.

A good friend told me about a time when she taught her son. During their drive home from church, one son got mad at his brother. He got so mad that he called him foul names. Mom was mortified and angry. As they pulled up to the house she told the offending son that she was so angry that she didn't trust herself right then to respond to him appropriately. She asked him to go to his room to settle down while she went to hers. He was worried.

After giving herself a moment to soothe her anger and pray, Mom went to her son's room. He was very humble. (He may also have been afraid for his life!) She explained to him why the language he had used was so troublesome to her. He apologized. She told him that he had offended two others: his brother and his Heavenly Father. With her help, he went and apologized to his brother. When they returned to his room, he asked how he could make things right with Heavenly Father.

That wise mom taught her son about prayer. They knelt together by the side of his bed and asked Father for forgiveness and help in doing better. That day he learned lasting lessons about the great principle of repentance. That mom was teaching her son.

Reflection:

Think of a time when you have patiently and lovingly taught your child. How did it feel?

_____

_____

What helped you get there? _____

_____

_____

How can you get there again? _____

_____

_____

How can you make that experience more common for you?_____

_____

_____

Applying this strategy:

☐ I ask Father for help.

☐ I remember (with gratitude) past successes with this strategy.

☐ I ask myself, does this strategy fit me? If not, can I adapt it or should I discard it?

☐ I plan my response for next time the challenge arises.

☐ I imagine or pre-experience the better way of responding.

☐ I try it out.

☐ I keep refining my efforts—otherwise known as repenting.

Notes on my progress: _____

_____

_____

_____

_____

_____

_____

35. Give fair warning.

Haim Ginott made an astute observation about parental anger: "When we lose our temper, we act as though we have lost our sanity. We say and do things to our children that we would hesitate to inflict on an enemy. We yell, insult, and hit below the belt. When the fanfare is over, we feel guilty and we solemnly resolve never to render a repeat performance. But anger soon strikes again, undoing our good intentions. Once more we lash out at those to whose welfare we have dedicated our life and fortune."[47]

Ginott made recommendations for preventing the devastation of anger. He suggested that we express our irritation without attacking the child's personality or character. We can say things like:

"I feel annoyed."

"I feel irritated."

"I am filled with indignation."

Sometimes just the statement of our feelings stops the bothersome behavior. Sometimes we may need to give more detail:

"When I see shoes, socks and shirts spread all over the floor, I get frustrated. I'm tempted to yell. I feel like opening the window and throwing the whole mess into the middle of the street."

"It makes me upset to see you hit your brother. I can never allow you to hurt him."

---

47 Haim Ginott, *Between Parent and Child* (New York: Three Rivers Press, 2003), 47.

"When I see all of you rush away from dinner to watch TV, and leave me with the dirty dishes and greasy pans, I feel upset! I fume inside! I need some help."

"When I call you for dinner and you don't come, I feel indignant. I say to myself, 'I cooked a good meal and I want some appreciation, not frustration.'"

Soft-spoken parents can be clear about their feelings without losing their tempers or attacking children. In fact, one of the best ways of preventing irrational anger is the expression of irritation long before it grows into anger.

Reflection:

Think of a time when you have given fair warning—when you have expressed irritation before it became anger.

How did it feel? _____

_____

_____

What helped you get there? _____

_____

_____

How can you get there again? _____

_____

_____

How can you make that experience more common for you?_____

_____

_____

Applying this strategy:

☐ I ask Father for help.
☐ I remember (with gratitude) past successes with this strategy.

☐ I ask myself, does this strategy fit me? If not, can I adapt it or should I discard it?

☐ I plan my response for next time the challenge arises.

☐ I imagine or pre-experience the better way of responding.

☐ I try it out.

☐ I keep refining my efforts—otherwise known as repenting.

Notes on my progress: _____

_____

_____

_____

_____

_____

_____

36. Keep the ratio right.

John Gottman[48] may be the world's leading marriage researcher. In his extensive studies of couples, he has found a magic ratio. In relationships that are strong, there are five positives for each negative. If you want a strong relationship, it is not enough to deliver one positive for each negative. It takes five positives for each negative. That is one of the best ways to assure a strong and enduring relationship.

Virginia Williams has applied this same idea to raising children. She suggests that many children hear a steady stream of complaints, accusations, and animosity. The children who become healthy adults are more likely to grow in a lake of support, encouragement, and appreciation.

If we monitored our messages to our children, I'm afraid that most of us would fall short of the magic ratio. Many of us deliver far too many corrections, irritations, and reprimands. Children may be crushed under the weight of our negativity.

Yet we can repent. We can be more mindful of the climate of our relationship with each child. We can offer more sunshine than storm. We can take our frustrations out on exercise rather than on our children. We can look for the good and talk about it.

Our goal is to have five positives for each negative.

Reflection:

Think of a time when you have given far more positives than negatives to each of your children.

---

48 Gottman's best books include *The 7 Principles for Making Marriage Work* and *Why Marriages Succeed or Fail.*

How did it feel? _____

_____

_____

What helped you get there? _____

_____

_____

How can you get there again? _____

_____

_____

How can you make that experience more common for you?_____

_____

_____

Applying this strategy:

☐ I ask Father for help.

☐ I remember (with gratitude) past successes with this strategy.

☐ I ask myself, does this strategy fit me? If not, can I adapt it or should I discard it?

☐ I plan my response for next time the challenge arises.

☐ I imagine or pre-experience the better way of responding.

☐ I try it out.

☐ I keep refining my efforts—otherwise known as repenting.

Notes on my progress: _____

_____

_____

_____

_____

_____

_____

37. Learn your children's languages of love.

There is a trick to loving children effectively. Effective loving requires us to deliver what is important to the specific child we are loving. It is not enough to say, "I love you!"—even with gusto. We can tell a daughter that she is loved, but she may prefer that you play with her. We can tell our son he is loved, but he may prefer that you throw the ball with him. One child might want snuggling while another loves story time. Each child is different.

This complex challenge could almost seem discouraging—except there are such wonderful and natural ways to discover each child's native love language. Very often children tell us exactly what they want:

"Please listen to me!"
"Hurry! Come see the bug outside!"
"Will you read me a story?"
"Are you mad at me?"

In every request is a hint about that child's needs and interests. In every question is also a cry for reassurance.

Ginott tells a great story about 6-year-old Flora who complained that she had not been receiving as many presents as her brother. Mother did not argue with Flora's perception. She did not pull out her check register to prove otherwise. She did not justify any differences saying that her brother was older and so deserved more presents. A wise mother knew that children are more concerned about the relationship than about the size and number of gifts. Mother simply said, "You wonder if I love you as much as him?" Without adding another word, mother hugged little Flora, who responded with a smile of surprise and pleasure. This was the right answer to a question that could have become an endless argument.

Flora wanted to be reassured that she was loved. Her mother was astute enough to recognize the real question behind the complaint. Mom answered the real question.

We can deliver the message in the way that works for each child. How can we know what each child wants? We can notice what each child asks for. We can notice how each child tends to show love. And we can notice what we have done in the past that seemed to be an effective message of love for that child.

I like to say that there are three particular languages of love and two universal ones.[49] The universal languages are taking time and being understanding. When someone spends time with us doing something we love to do, that sends a clear message of love. As to being understanding, when someone takes the time to really understand my feelings, I am warmed and comforted by that person's love and goodness.

The three particular languages of love are: show me, tell me, and touch me. Some children are only convinced that we love them when they see our actions. Some are dying to hear (or read) words of love. Others want to snuggle.

Of course every person has some unique combination of love languages. And they change from time to time. A child who is lonely and tired may want to snuggle even though that is not usually her language of love.

When Nephi teaches us that God "speaketh unto men according to their language, unto their understanding," I wonder if God doesn't expect us to do the same thing for our children—to learn their languages of love.

---

49 See www.arfamilies.org for more information about these languages of love.

Reflection:

Think of a time when you have shown love to each of your children in a way that really communicated to that child.

How did it feel? _____

_____

_____

What helped you get there? _____

_____

_____

How can you get there again? _____

_____

_____

How can you make that experience more common for you?_____

_____

_____

Applying this strategy:

☐ I ask Father for help.

☐ I remember (with gratitude) past successes with this strategy.

☐ I ask myself, does this strategy fit me? If not, can I adapt it or should I discard it?

☐ I plan my response for next time the challenge arises.

☐ I imagine or pre-experience the better way of responding.

☐ I try it out.

☐ I keep refining my efforts—otherwise known as repenting.

Notes on my progress: _____

_____

_____

Learn your children's languages of love.

_____

_____

_____

_____

38. Share with other parents.

We seem to assume that parenting should just come naturally. We surely don't want to admit to friends or neighbors that we are bewildered or vexed by the challenges of raising children.

What a crazy assumption! Nothing is more challenging than parenting. It is one of the most challenging courses God offers in preparation for eternity. It is extraordinarily rare for anyone to make an A in this course!

Yet we do not attend lectures, hold study groups, or read books to help us pass the tests of parenting. No wonder that we fail so many parenting tests!

I recommend that *every* parent do several things:

1. Read the best books on parenting.[50] Following are some suggestions:

Between Parent and Child by Haim Ginott
Raising an Emotionally Intelligent Child by John Gottman
How to Talk So Kids will Listen and Listen So Kids Will Talk by Adele Faber and Elaine Mazlish
What to Expect the First Year by Arlene Eisenberg and associates
Dr. Spock's Baby and Child Care by Benjamin Spock and Michael Rothenberg

2. Take good classes when they are offered.

Unfortunately, there are far more poor books and classes than good ones. How can you tell the difference? Generally, the best ones are sponsored by universities or other groups that are less commercial and more research-based. Also, the best ones encourage you to show love to your children while

---

50 For recommended books on special issues, see *Authoritative Guide to Self-Help Resources in Mental Health* (New York: The Guilford Press, 2000).

helping them cultivate their agency. Any program that encourages harsh or manipulative parenting should be avoided. Be cautious about any programs that offer sure cures. God doesn't offer simple, guaranteed formulas. God always requires us to use wisdom and inspiration. Any parenting guru who offers sure cures is unwise and probably hawking a poor program.

3. Interview parents you respect.

You probably know some parents who seem to have a knack for raising children. Interview them. Ask them what they have learned. Ask them how they deal with challenging situations. You might even set up a discussion group to share ideas among conscientious parents.

4. Study Heavenly Father's perfect example of parenting.

Heavenly Father is the Perfect Parent. The scriptures are nothing but the dealings of the Perfect Parent with his struggling children. As we study Father's wise and loving ways, we can learn vital lessons about how to be better parents.

5. Plea for Heavenly help.

We cannot raise children effectively without heavenly help. I recommend that all of us use the "have mercy" plea daily. (See Strategy 30.)

With some effort we might create a learning culture—one where we don't expect anyone to have all the answers but where we work together to draw heavenly wisdom into the challenges of parenting. The successful parent is the one who keeps working to find better ways. As we get better ideas for parenting, we are less likely to use poor ones—like anger.

Reflection:

Think of a time when you have gained from sharing with other parents. What helped you get there? _____

_____

_____

How can you get there again? _____

_____

_____

Is there anything you can do do make that experience more common for you? _____

_____

_____

Applying this strategy:

☐ I ask Father for help.

☐ I remember (with gratitude) past successes with this strategy.

☐ I ask myself, does this strategy fit me? If not, can I adapt it or should I discard it?

☐ I plan my response for next time the challenge arises.

☐ I imagine or pre-experience the better way of responding.

☐ I try it out.

☐ I keep refining my efforts—otherwise known as repenting.

Notes on my progress: _____

_____

_____

_____

_____

_____

39. Strive for God's perspective.

We simply don't see things the way God does. Joseph Smith taught, "While one portion of the human race is judging and condemning the other without mercy, the Great Parent of the universe looks upon the whole of the human family with a fatherly care and paternal regard; he views them as his offspring, and without any of those contracted feelings that influence the children of men...we shall all of us eventually have to confess that the Judge of all the earth has done right.[51]

Our tendency as mortal parents is to judge and condemn our children. As we cultivate "fatherly care and paternal regard," we are more likely to be soft-spoken parents.

Richard L. Evans observed that "our Father in heaven is not an umpire who is trying to count us out. He is not a competitor who is trying to outsmart us. He is not a prosecutor who is trying to convict us. He is a Loving Father who wants our happiness and eternal progress and everlasting opportunity and glorious accomplishment, and who will help us all he can if we will but give him, in our lives, the opportunity to do so with obedience and humility and faith and patience."[52]

Our challenge is to be like Father, wanting the happiness and eternal progress or our children. How do we cultivate this heavenly perspective? There are many skills we can learn. But after all the skills are mastered, the most effective way to become more godlike in our parenting is to be filled with him, to have the mighty change of heart, to have the mind of Christ.

---

51 Joseph Smith, *History of the Church* 4:595–96.
52 *Conference Report*, October 1956, 101.

This is the work of a lifetime. We continue to struggle day after day and year after year. We continue to make mistakes. We wish we had better parenting to bring to our children. But our very model of repentance and growth is a great gift to them.

So we strive to see our children as God sees them and see their possibilities as God sees them. As we get the mind and heart of Christ, our parenting becomes wiser, finer, and kinder. President Ezra Taft Benson taught:

> Men and women who turn their lives over to God will discover that he can make a lot more out of their lives than they can. He will deepen their joys, expand their vision, quicken their minds, strengthen their muscles, lift their spirits, multiply their blessings, increase their opportunities, comfort their souls, raise up friends, and pour out peace. Whoever will lose his life in the service of God will find eternal life.[53]

When we turn our lives over to God, he will also make us better parents.

Reflection:

Think of a time when you have had God's perspective on your children. How did it feel?

_____

_____

What helped you get there? _____

_____

_____

---

53 *The Teachings of Ezra Taft Benson* (Salt Lake City: Bookcraft, 1988), 361.

Strive for God's perspective.

How can you get there again? _____

_____

How can you make that experience more common for you? _____

_____

_____

Applying this strategy:

☐ I ask Father for help.

☐ I remember (with gratitude) past successes with this strategy.

☐ I ask myself, does this strategy fit me? If not, can I adapt it or should I discard it?

☐ I plan my response for next time the challenge arises.

☐ I imagine or pre-experience the better way of responding.

☐ I try it out.

☐ I keep refining my efforts—otherwise known as repenting.

Notes on my progress: _____

_____

_____

_____

_____

_____

_____

40. Set yourself up for success.

We often set ourselves and our children up for failure. We expect perfect performance. We don't allow time for unexpected challenges. We drag loads of irritation from all areas of life around with us. It's no wonder that we blow up.

We can choose instead to set ourselves up for success. John Covey told me about coming home from work feeling tired. Before he entered the house to greet Jane and their children, he paused in the car and prayed. He asked Father for the energy and goodness to enter family life as a source of light.

The prayer for greater goodness can set us up for success. So can the wisdom to make allowances for unexpected challenges and childish balkiness. We can also be sure we call on help from friends or family when we are dealing with extra challenges.

Reflection:

Think of a time when you have set yourself and your children up for success. How did it feel? _____

_____

_____

What helped you get there? _____

_____

_____

How can you get there again? _____

_____

_____

How can you make that experience more common for you? _____
_____
_____

Applying this strategy:

☐ I ask Father for help.

☐ I remember (with gratitude) past successes with this strategy.

☐ I ask myself, does this strategy fit me? If not, can I adapt it or should I discard it?

☐ I plan my response for next time the challenge arises.

☐ I imagine or pre-experience the better way of responding.

☐ I try it out.

☐ I keep refining my efforts—otherwise known as repenting.

Notes on my progress: _____
_____
_____
_____
_____
_____
_____

41. Change your view of children and human nature.

We all make certain assumptions about people and the reasons they do the things they do. We call this an implicit personality theory. Tucked away in our personal theories are ideas about the basic goodness and badness of people. Here are voices of three different views of human nature:

1. Children are basically bad.

John Calvin (16th Century): Children's whole nature is a certain seed of Sin, therefore it cannot but be hateful and abominable to God.[54]

Sigmund Freud (19th and 20th Centuries): I have found little that is good about human beings. In my experience most of them are trash…. In the depths of my heart, I can't help being convinced that my dear fellowmen, with few exceptions, are worthless.[55]

Anna Freud (20th Century): From birth onwards, children feel the pressure of urgent body needs and powerful instinctive urges (such as hunger, sex, aggression) which clamor for satisfaction.[56]

John Rosemond (20th and 21st Centuries): Give your children regular and realistic doses of Vitamin N ("no"). When you do, and they fall to the floor screaming, pat yourself on the back for a job well done. Remember that sufficient exposure to frustration not only prepares a child for the reality of adulthood, but gradually helps the child develop a tolerance for frustration.[57]

54 Quoted from A. Synnott, "Little angels, little devils: A sociology of children," *Canadian Review of Sociology and Anthropology*, 20(1), (1983), 79–95.

55 R. Byrne, *1911 Best Things Anybody Ever Said* (New York: Fawcett Columbine, 1988), 194, and A.M. Nicholi, *The Question of God* (New York: Free Press, 2002), 181.

56 D. Beekman, *The Mechanical Baby* (Chicago: Chicago Review Press, 1977), 188.

57 J. Rosemond, *John Rosemond's Six-Point Plan for Raising Happy, Healthy Children* (New York: Andrews & McMeel, 1989), 190.

This is a very dismal view of human nature. And it is a good description of the natural man. Yet it is at odds with God's description of children as innocent (D&C 93:38–39).

2. Children are clay.

Aristotle (300 BC): The soul of a child is like a clean slate on which nothing is written, on it you may write what you will.[58]

John B. Watson (20ᵗʰ Century): Give me a dozen healthy infants, well-formed, and my own specified world to bring them up in and I'll guarantee to take any one at random and train him to become any type of specialist I might select—into a doctor, lawyer, artist, merchant-chief, and yes, even into beggar-man and thief, regardless of his talents, penchants, tendencies, abilities, vocations and race of ancestors.[59]

This view assumes that children are merely mercenaries. You can get them to do anything with the right reward. It certainly does not explain all of human nature. Could we have turned Joseph Smith or any of the prophets into vile sinners by regularly rewarding bad behavior? I don't think so.

3. Children are good, innocent, angelic.

Jean Jacques Rousseau (18ᵗʰ Century): All things are good as they come out of the hands of the Creator, but everything degenerates in the hands of man.[60]

Harry Emerson Fosdick (20ᵗʰ Century): Every exaltation, every pure sentiment, all urgency of true affection, and all yearning after things higher and nobler, are testimonies of the divinity that is in us.[61]

---

58 Quoted from D. Beekman, *The Mechanical Baby* (Chicago: Chicago Review Press, 1977), 20.
59 J. B. Watson, *Psychological Care of Infant and Child* (New York: W. W. Norton, 1928), 41.
60 Quoted from D. Beekman, *The Mechanical Baby* (Chicago: Chicago Review Press, 1977), 47.
61 Harry Emerson Fosdick, *The Meaning of Faith* (New York: Association Press, 1918), 89.

Abraham Maslow (20ᵗʰ Century): If one looks at a healthy and well-loved and cared-for infant…then it is quite impossible to see anything that could be called evil…. On the contrary, careful and long-continued observation demonstrates the opposite. Practically every personality characteristic found in [the most exemplary] people, everything lovable, admirable, and enviable is found in babies.[62]

These quotes represent three different views of children. Our view of children and their nature affects the way we treat them. While they may act basically bad when they are tired and frustrated and may act like clay when they want something from us, the most interesting and powerful part of human nature is the divine within them. They are children of God! Eternity and divinity are written in their genetics.

So, when children are cranky, we soothe them. When they act like little mercenaries, we make sure we are not rewarding bad behavior. But the heart of effective parenting is encouraging the holiness in each child. The Lord commands us to bring them up in light and truth! (D&C 93:40)

Francine Bennion provides a good example of a child who might be seen as bad but, when rightly understood, was a model of goodness.[63] The family lived in a farm area that was suffering from serious drought. This drought was devastating for families in the area. The local ward held a fast for rain and asked that all pray for rain in their evening prayers.

That evening little Lynne asked in her prayer for rain so the crops would grow. Her mother tucked her into bed and went to the kitchen, expecting Lynne to go right to sleep. But half an hour later, mother heard the front door open and close. She looked to see the reason and saw Lynne in her nightgown picking up toys from the front lawn and putting them in her wagon.

---

62 A. H. Maslow, *Motivation and Personality* (New York: Harper & Row 1954/1970), 118, 122.
63 Francine Bennion, "Stone or Bread?" *Ensign*, January 1976, 38.

"Lynne, come in here!" mother called. "What are you doing?"

"Just bringing in my toys, Mommy, so they won't get wet when it rains tonight."

And during the night, the rain came.

When we look for divine goodness in children, we are likely to both find it and encourage it.

Reflection:

Think of a time when you have taken a positive view of your children. How did it feel? _____

_____

_____

What helped you get there? _____

_____

_____

How can you get there again? _____

_____

_____

How can you make that experience more common for you?_____

_____

_____

Applying this strategy:

☐ I ask Father for help.
☐ I remember (with gratitude) past successes with this strategy.
☐ I ask myself, does this strategy fit me? If not, can I adapt it or should I discard it?

☐ I plan my response for next time the challenge arises.

☐ I imagine or pre-experience the better way of responding.

☐ I try it out.

☐ I keep refining my efforts—otherwise known as repenting.

Notes on my progress: _____

_____

_____

_____

_____

_____

_____

42. Use persuasion.

Joseph F. Smith had a unique perspective on parenting. He lost his dear and beloved father when he was only 5. He lost his exemplary and faith-filled mother when he was only 13. Those losses seem to have made him more tender. Consider his counsel:

> Get [your children] to feel as you feel, have interest in the things in which you take interest, to love the gospel as you love it, to love one another as you love them; to love their parents as the parents love the children. You can't do it any other way. You can't do it by unkindness; you cannot do it by driving; our children are like we are; we couldn't be driven; we can't be driven now. We are like some other animals that we know of in the world. You can coax them; you can lead them, by holding out inducements to them, and by speaking kindly to them, but you can't drive them; they won't be driven. We won't be driven. Men are not in the habit of being driven; they are not made that way.[64]

What sweet counsel!

Similarly, the Lord counsels us to exert influence by "persuasion, by long-suffering, by gentleness and meekness, and by love unfeigned" (D&C 121:41). Persuasion is the way of heaven.

As if the counsel of God and his prophets were not enough, all this agrees with the discoveries of decades of research on parenting. The best way to influence children is with a method we call induction.[65] When we reason

---

64 *Gospel Doctrine: Selections from the Sermons and Writings of Joseph F. Smith*, ed. John A. Widtsoe (Salt Lake City: Deseret Book, 1939), 316.

65 See B. C. Rollins and D. L. Thomas, "Parental Support, Power, and Control Techniques in the Socialization of Children." *Contemporary Theories about The Family, Volume I*. ed.W. R. Burr, R. Hill, R. I. Nye, & I. L. Reiss (New York: Free Press, 1979), 317–364.

with children and help then understand how their behavior affects others, they are more likely to become strong and caring adults.

There is a way in which this point is commonly misunderstood. Some parents feel that they must continue to cajole and beg their children until their children agree with them. They seem very intimidated about the prospect of having their children unhappy with them. This is not persuasion. This is intimidation by children.

Just as God does not change his laws when we have a fit, so the wise parent works to educate a child without giving in to a child's browbeating.

Reflection:

Think of a time when you have used persuasion with one of your children. How did it feel? _____

_____

_____

What helped you get there? _____

_____

_____

How can you get there again? _____

_____

_____

How can you make that experience more common for you?_____

_____

_____

Use persuasion.

Applying this strategy:

☐ I ask Father for help.

☐ I remember (with gratitude) past successes with this strategy.

☐ I ask myself, does this strategy fit me? If not, can I adapt it or should I discard it?

☐ I plan my response for next time the challenge arises.

☐ I imagine or pre-experience the better way of responding.

☐ I try it out.

☐ I keep refining my efforts—otherwise known as repenting.

Notes on my progress: _____

_____

_____

_____

_____

_____

_____

43. Invest 5 minutes to save an hour.

My esteemed colleague, Karen DeBord, suggests that parents can often invest 5 minutes to save an hour. This is especially true when we have been away from our children for an hour or more. They miss us. If we invest a few minutes reading, cuddling, listening, talking, walking, or rocking, we may save an evening of battles—and a lifetime of distance.

Nancy knew how to use this principle with our dear daughter, Sara, when she was a teen. When Nancy wanted to connect with Sara, she knew that she could not just offer a quick hello or a few words of affection. It takes a few minutes to reconnect.

So Nancy would take Sara with her to run errands. As they rode along in the car, Sara moved from superficial talk to cautious probing to soul sharing. It was simply the best way to reconnect with Sara.

A good mom in Montgomery, Alabama, once asked me how to deal with her sullen teen. The girl was often disagreeable, but when she first came home from school each day she wanted to spend some time hugging her mama. The mom was okay with a quick hug. But the daughter wanted to hang on. It drove the mother crazy. She had much to do. She figured a quick hug should do the job.

I encouraged the mother to mentally plan to take a few minutes to hug her daughter any time the daughter wanted a hug. Just be there. Take as many minutes as the daughter wanted.

The mother tried it. She discovered two surprises. First, contrary to expectation, the daughter did not lean on her for hours. After only a minute or two, the daughter was happy and went about her business. The second surprise was that those few minutes made a real difference in the quality of the rest of hours of the day.

As the Spanish proverb observes, "An ounce of mother is worth a ton of priest."

Reflection:

Think of a time when you have invested a few minutes to reconnect with one of your children.

How did it feel? _____

_____

_____

What helped you make the investment? _____

_____

_____

How can you do it again? _____

_____

_____

How can you make that experience more common for you? _____

_____

_____

Applying this strategy:

☐ I ask Father for help.

☐ I remember (with gratitude) past successes with this strategy.

☐ I ask myself, does this strategy fit me? If not, can I adapt it or should I discard it?

☐ I plan my response for next time the challenge arises.

☐ I imagine or pre-experience the better way of responding.

☐ I try it out.

☐ I keep refining my efforts—otherwise known as repenting.

Notes on my progress: _____

_____

_____

_____

_____

_____

_____

44. Make repairs.

We all get mad. We all hurt each other. We all have regular need of repentance.

One evening after family home evening, my daughter Sara and I were competing at some game. Sara is very good at games. But I was quite determined to do my best in this competition. I wanted to win.

In the process I was not very kind. When Sara's feeling were hurt, I blamed her for starting a game she wasn't willing to lose. Each of us felt offended by the other.

I did not sleep well that night. In the middle of the night I wandered to the living room and sat in the hint of moonlight rocking in a chair. When sleep would not come, I chose to use the time to pray. I asked Father the stewardship questions[66] including, "Father, what do I need to do to be a better family member."

Immediately the experience with Sara earlier that evening came to mind. I realized that I needed to repent and ask Sara's forgiveness. Since she was long-since asleep, I put a chair in the hall outside her room, placed a teddy bear on the chair, and left a note in the hands of the bear telling her how sorry I was that I had been unkind. I love Sara more than life itself and know I am foolish when I let anything blind me to that love. I told her just that.

All of us have occasion to repent. Our children will respect and love us more as they witness us repent of our follies. In addition, they will become better repenters themselves.

---

66 See Stephen Covey's excellent "Educated Conscience," *Speeches*, 27 May 1975, Brigham Young University, http://speeches.byu.edu/index.php?act=viewitem&id=948

Reflection:

Think of a time when you have used repentance to make repairs in a relationship with one of your children.

How did it feel? _____

_____

_____

What helped you get there? _____

_____

_____

How can you get there again? _____

_____

_____

How can you make that experience more common for you?_____

_____

_____

Applying this strategy:

☐ I ask Father for help.

☐ I remember (with gratitude) past successes with this strategy.

☐ I ask myself, does this strategy fit me? If not, can I adapt it or should I discard it?

☐ I plan my response for next time the challenge arises.

☐ I imagine or pre-experience the better way of responding.

☐ I try it out.

☐ I keep refining my efforts—otherwise known as repenting.

Notes on my progress: _____

_____

_____

_____

45. Give choices.   ☐ ☑ ☐

One of the primary objectives of good parenting is teaching children how to use their agency wisely. We don't accomplish that purpose when we make all their decisions for them. We also don't help them when we leave them to make decisions for which they are not prepared. For that reason, one of our family mottoes is:

> It is our job to help our children get what they want in a way we feel good about.

Notice the two parts of this formula: 1) We want to help them get what they want. We want them to have experience, growth, and lots of freedom; 2) We should set bounds on their decisions so they are not required to make decisions for which they are not prepared. Just as we must learn to act within the bounds the Lord has set, so we should teach our children to act within the bounds we have set.

Tommy was sitting on my lap as I read a book to him. After we had read for a while he seemed to become bored. He got a pencil and looked like he was going to write in the book. His dad jumped at him, grabbed the pencil, and shouted, "You do not write in books!" Both Tommy and I were shocked.

I think it would have been more helpful to give Tommy a choice. The father could ask him: "Would you like to draw? We don't draw in books but I can get you some paper to draw on. Or would you like to finish the book?" Either choice would have been fine.[67]

Sometimes children resist us because we try to force them to do things. When we do not give them choices, they are more likely to rebel. A young

---

67 This story is adapted from *The Frightful and Joyous Journey of Family Life* by the author.

child may resist going to bed. We may try to force the child. But they can resist us with calls for water, and a light, and a story. We can hurl angry lectures and threats at them.

It may be better to give choices. We might ask, "Would you like daddy or mommy to tuck you in?" or "Would you like to pick a storybook for me to read to you or would you like me to pick one?" If the child says that she does not want to go to bed, we can ask the same question. She has a choice within boundaries set by her parents. We can be perfectly pleasant while being totally firm.

Of course we should only give children choices when we feel that either choice is acceptable. We do not let a small child decide to play with knives or run into traffic. Adult wisdom should frame choices for children. But we should allow children to pick the shirt they will wear even if it has a bit of mustard on it.

As children become teens, many conflicts arise out of difference in taste. We interpret their style in clothes or music to suggest disrespect or rebellion. Sometimes it does. Often it does not.

In matters of style, it is better not to start a battle. We may think our child's hair is too long or too short or that baggy pants look ridiculous. (Probably our parents had some of the same concerns about our style.) We allow our children freedom to express themselves in ways that are not unsafe or immoral. We try not to panic when some of those choices are different from ones we would make.

It is not helpful to pester children, but we can help them learn sensible ways of making choices. If we want our children to be good decision-makers when they become adults, we should give them many appropriate opportunities to make decisions along their journey to adulthood.

When Andy seemed to play music from the band U2 endlessly, I was tempted to tell him to shut off his stinking music. Instead, I gave him a choice. I asked if he would rather play the music quietly or use headsets. (The irony is that I now own and enjoy several U2 albums.)

If we want our children to become good decision-makers, we should give them lots of chances to make choices.

Reflection:

Think of a time when you have appropriately allowed your children to make choices.

How did it feel? _____

_____

_____

What helped you get there? _____

_____

_____

How can you get there again? _____

_____

_____

How can you make that experience more common for you?_____

_____

_____

Applying this strategy:

☐ I ask Father for help.

☐ I remember (with gratitude) past successes with this strategy.

☐ I ask myself, does this strategy fit me? If not, can I adapt it or should I discard it?

☐ I plan my response for next time the challenge arises.

☐ I imagine or pre-experience the better way of responding.
☐ I try it out.
☐ I keep refining my efforts—otherwise known as repenting.

Notes on my progress: _____

_____

_____

_____

_____

_____

_____

46. Point them to God.

Francine Bennion told a story that has always touched my heart.[68] In it she tells of a celebration in July in which family and friends met for a picnic at a local lake. Members of the group walked around the lake to a three-walled rectangular shelter complete with roof and two wooden tables. The structure included a metal-covered cement stove on which to cook hot dogs and hamburgers.

As the group gathered, the sky darkened. A violent thunderstorm came up. Suddenly an awful spear of lightning and explosion of thunder struck the chimney and exploded the stove. Sister Bennion described it: "Pieces of cement flew into bare arms, children were thrown against walls, purple-brown lines streaked down necks to ankles."

No one was killed or seriously injured, but a question exploded from Francine: "I thought Heavenly Father would take care of us?" Why hadn't they been protected? She reports that her mother came into the rain answering her question, "What do you think he did?"

Indeed. Usually when we feel betrayed, we might well ask ourselves, "What would have happened if God had not been protecting us?" Instead of minor injuries, there might have been deaths. Instead of serene loss, there might have been senseless tragedy.

Francine Bennion's mother pointed her daughter to God at a critical time. Her experience reminds me of dear friends in Provo who were enjoying a picnic up a canyon when a tree was blown over killing the grandmother and crippling a daughter. Yet, the faith-filled example of the parents points the

---

68 Francine Bennion, "A Large and Reasonable Context," *A Thoughtful Faith: Essays on Belief by Mormon Scholars* ed. P. L. Barlow (Centerville, UT: Canon Press, 1986), 103–116.

children to God: "Father was looking over us. We are so grateful to him!" As Job expressed, "the Lord gave, and the Lord hath taken away; blessed be the name of the Lord."

Each of us will have thousands of opportunities to help our children see faith in action. Rather than becoming bitter and resentful, we can teach our children to trust in the Lord.

Reflection:

Think of a time when you have pointed your children to God.
How did it feel? _____

_____

_____

What helped you get there? _____

_____

_____

How can you get there again? _____

_____

_____

How can you make that experience more common for you?_____

_____

_____

Applying this strategy:

☐ I ask Father for help.
☐ I remember (with gratitude) past successes with this strategy.
☐ I ask myself, does this strategy fit me? If not, can I adapt it or should I discard it?
☐ I plan my response for next time the challenge arises.
☐ I imagine or pre-experience the better way of responding.

Point them to God.

☐ I try it out.

☐ I keep refining my efforts—otherwise known as repenting.

Notes on my progress: _____

_____

_____

_____

_____

_____

_____

47. Turn it over to a rule.

It is quite possible to have endless battles over trivial matters. For example, how many arguments have there been over coats since Mother Eve told Seth to bundle up and button up when he went out to play? We describe the catastrophes that await children who do not dress warmly. Yet children insist that they are not cold.

It does not make sense to argue with someone else's perception. How can we settle this timeless battle?

One method is to let a rule speak for itself. Maybe we make the rule that a jacket or coat must be worn if the temperature is under 50 degrees. As a child is dashing out the door to school, we can remind the child to grab a coat. If they resist, we point them to the rule: "Check the thermometer. Over 50, you decide. Under 50, wrap up tight."

In many cases we can let consequences teach children. Mother nature is one of the best teachers in the universe. A child who doesn't wear a coat may get chilly. A child who refuses sunscreen may get sunburned. We can let her do a lot of the teaching. A healthy child is likely to survive outdoor play in temperatures that might bother us.

In situations where there are genuine safety concerns, we can point children to simple rules.

Reflection:

Think of a time when you have pointed your children to a simple rule.

How did it feel? _____

_____

_____

What helped you get there? _____

_____

_____

How can you get there again? _____

_____

_____

How can you make that experience more common for you?_____

_____

_____

Applying this strategy:

☐ I ask Father for help.

☐ I remember (with gratitude) past successes with this strategy.

☐ I ask myself, does this strategy fit me? If not, can I adapt it or should I discard it?

☐ I plan my response for next time the challenge arises.

☐ I imagine or pre-experience the better way of responding.

☐ I try it out.

☐ I keep refining my efforts—otherwise known as repenting.

Notes on my progress: _____

_____

_____

_____

_____

_____

48. Respond to anger with compassion.

"If we practice an eye for an eye and a tooth for a tooth, soon we will all be blind and toothless," Mahatma Gandhi observed. Jesus asked us to live by a higher standard than the Law of Moses: "But I say unto you, Love your enemies, bless them that curse you, do good to them that hate you, and pray for them which despitefully use you, and persecute you" (Matthew 5:44).

Jesus also modeled the lofty standard he preached. He taught those who attacked him and prayed for those who crucified him.

What a challenge to follow his example in our parenting. When our children are upset with us, we don't have to become defensive. We can show compassion for their pain.

John Gottman tells the story of flying home from a visit with relatives with his daughter, 2-year-old Moriah, who was bored, tired, and cranky.[69] Moriah asked for Zebra, her favorite stuffed animal. Unfortunately Zebra was packed in the suitcase in the hold of the plane.

John explained to his tired girl that he could not get Zebra—that he was in a suitcase under the plane.

Did Moriah say to herself, "Too bad. I'm disappointed, but I might as well relax"? No. She whined pitifully for her stuffed animal.

Once again Dad explained the situation and apologized. Moriah's moans turned to screams. "I want Zebra! I want Zebra!"

---

69 John Gottman, *Raising an Emotionally Intelligent Child,* (New York: Simon and Schuster, 1998), 69–70.

At this point many of us are tempted to lose our cool. We have been civil, why can't the child be civil? In fact, her dad's blood pressure was rising. He explained again and offered another toy. Moriah got more upset.

Out of desperation, Gottman turned to the very thing he recommends to parents. He offered her compassion. He moved out of his defenses into her yearning. "You wish you had Zebra right now."

"Yeah," replied Moriah.

"You're tired and you would like to snuggle with Zebra and feel him against your face. You'd like to get out of these seats and climb into your big, soft bed full of all your stuffed animals."

"Yeah."

"I wish we could, too. I would love to snuggle with you and read you a story like we often do." Moriah began to relax. Soon she was asleep.

Gottman followed Ginott's wise prescription: Grant in fantasy what you cannot grant in reality. Gottman could not get Zebra for Moriah. And Moriah did not want explanations. She wanted compassion. When Dad stopped pushing back on her request and stood with her (emotionally) to understand her request, she became more peaceful.

Reflection:

Think of a time when you have responded to a child's anger with compassion.
How did it feel? _____

_____

_____

What helped you get there? _____

_____

_____

How can you get there again? _____

_____

_____

How can you make that experience more common for you?_____

_____

_____

Applying this strategy:

- ☐ I ask Father for help.
- ☐ I remember (with gratitude) past successes with this strategy.
- ☐ I ask myself, does this strategy fit me? If not, can I adapt it or should I discard it?
- ☐ I plan my response for next time the challenge arises.
- ☐ I imagine or pre-experience the better way of responding.
- ☐ I try it out.
- ☐ I keep refining my efforts—otherwise known as repenting.

Notes on my progress: _____

_____

_____

_____

_____

_____

_____

49. Make allowance for childishness.

It is natural—but not helpful—for us to impose grown-up expectations on little people. Haim Ginott recommends that we accept the childishness of children.[70] This means accepting that "a clean shirt on a normal child will not stay clean for long, that running rather than walking is the child's normal means of locomotion, that a tree is for climbing and a mirror is for making faces."

A mother called Nancy and me one day because her 4-year-old girl was making her crazy. We asked for examples of the misbehavior that were upsetting Mama. Mom fumed, "Sometimes Julie leaves the hall light on in the day. Sometimes she even brings cookies into the living room."

Most of the "unpardonable sins" of childhood are merely a part of being a human—especially a human without a lot of experience. At what point in life should we expect people to reliably turn off the hall lights and leave cookies in the kitchen? I'm not sure. But it is a lot to ask of a 4-year-old.

Rather than get mad when Julie forgets to turn off the light, a parent might say, "Julie, it looks like you forgot the light. Do you mind turning it off?"

Rather than become indignant when Julie brings a cookie into the living room, we might invite: "Do you want me to join you in the kitchen while you eat your cookie? I'd love to be with you. Or you can leave it in the kitchen to eat later."

I remember when our Emily was a little girl. She asked me to draw a circle for her. I thought that was goofy: "You're a smart girl! You can draw a circle. Just think of a cookie and draw it." A few days later I read that drawing

---

70 Ginott, Haim G., *Between Parent and Child* (New York: Three Rivers Press, 2003), 117.

circles is something that some children can't do until they are much older than Emily was. I was not making allowances for childishness.

Childishness is not a bad thing—in children. When we sign up for parenting, we should expect that we will be doing a lot of teaching, reminding—and forgiving.

Reflection:

Think of a time when you have made allowances for childishness.
How did it feel? _____

_____

_____

What helped you get there? _____

_____

_____

How can you get there again? _____

_____

_____

How can you make that experience more common for you?_____

_____

_____

Applying this strategy:

☐ I ask Father for help.
☐ I remember (with gratitude) past successes with this strategy.
☐ I ask myself, does this strategy fit me? If not, can I adapt it or should I discard it?
☐ I plan my response for next time the challenge arises.
☐ I imagine or pre-experience the better way of responding.

☐ I try it out.

☐ I keep refining my efforts—otherwise known as repenting.

Notes on my progress: _____

_____

_____

_____

_____

_____

_____

50. Be strategic.

Sometimes we become anything but soft-spoken when children do not respond to our requests. And we may have acted without considering what would help the child move in the desired direction. Sometimes we get just what we should have expected.

I like the story about a woman who stepped out of the house to throw something in the trash. When she returned to the house, she found that she was locked out. Inside was her four-year-old son. She could demand that her son open the door immediately. We all know what would happen. There would be a battle of wills with Mom increasing threats and son resisting demands. The mother chose to be strategic. In a sad voice she said, "Oh, too bad. You just locked yourself in the house." The boy opened the door at once.

That is being strategic! Rather than doing things that we know won't work, we can do the things that will work.

For example, rushing and nagging children does not help them get ready for school on time. What is a more strategic approach? One mother told her sons that as soon as they were fully ready for school, they could watch cartoons until time to leave for school. A dad motivated his children by having a hot breakfast for those who were ready on time. Those who were not got a granola bar.

A parent who had a hard time getting children dressed could play the role of a salesperson. "Sir, are you looking for something to wear today? We have two lovely shirts to choose from. Does one appeal to you? Would you also like a handsome pair of pants? We have this snappy blue pair and a casual brown pair. Which of these appeals to you?" The parent continues until the child is dressed—and then can conclude: "Thank you for shopping with us today." A hug and laugh would be a fitting conclusion. Where this approach will work, it is certainly better than demanding and threatening.

A child who has a hard time sitting still in sacrament meeting might benefit from some strategic parenting. A parent might draw pictures of activities that the child could do in sacrament meeting and invite the child to plan sacrament meeting time. These could be placed on a clock face and could end up with a schedule like the following:

9:00 to 9:15	Picture book of Jesus
9:15 to 9:30	Quiet book or lift-a-flap book
9:30 to 9:50	Draw pictures of Nephi and the family making their journey
9:50 to 10:05	Scripture picture book

The child could help the parent pack the bag with supplies to take to church. Children are more likely to have a good church experience if they help plan their experience.

There is even a strategic way of dealing with tantrums. When a child has a meltdown, the parent can sit nearby and wait with perfect tranquility. The parent can even say, "I sure want to hear your feelings. I can't understand what you're saying right now. When you're ready, please tell me what you're feeling." Then the parent waits for the child to calm down.

A parent can get children to eat better by making an adventure of it. "That broccoli looks like a tree. What does it taste like?" Parents can also use or provide a cookie cutter to form interesting shapes. And we've all made ants on a log (peanut butter and raisins on celery). A child might also bring a stuffed animal to the table to "share" with.

Any one of these ideas—or all of them—might not work for a given child. Fortunately, you are an expert on your children. You can design the strategic approaches that will work with each of your children. Whether it is happy ways to get hair washed or methods to help them fall asleep, being strategic can often help us turn away confrontation and wrath.[71]

Reflection:

Think of a time when you have been strategic in dealing with your children. How did it feel? _____

_____

_____

What helped you get there? _____

_____

_____

How can you get there again? _____

_____

_____

How can you make that experience more common for you?_____

_____

_____

Applying this strategy:

☐ I ask Father for help.

☐ I remember (with gratitude) past successes with this strategy.

☐ I ask myself, does this strategy fit me? If not, can I adapt it or should I discard it?

☐ I plan my response for next time the challenge arises.

☐ I imagine or pre-experience the better way of responding.

---

71 For more ideas, see David Borgenicht & James Grace's *How to Con Your Kid* (Philadelphia: Quirk Books, 2005).

Be strategic.

☐ I try it out.
☐ I keep refining my efforts—otherwise known as repenting.

Notes on my progress: _____

_____

_____

_____

_____

_____

_____

51. Send a clear message.

Often we send mixed messages to our children. We say things like "You're a nice kid *but* why don't you clean up your room, do your chores, help your brother, etc.?" That is one big "but."

One Saturday morning I was standing with a friend in the entrance to his garage.[72] As we spoke, his young son rode into the garage on his bike and parked it in front of their old station wagon. Something about parking the bike there violated a family rule because the father interrupted our conversation to launch over to his son, grab him, hold him up in the air and start to yell the Standard Parental Lecture. "Why do you always...Why can't you ever...Won't you ever learn...What is it going to take..."

Let's leave our adult perspective and see the situation from the child's point of view. What do you think the son was thinking as he was suspended in mid-air with an angry face belching his mistakes? Do you think he was saying, "I am so glad that dad is bringing these things to my attention. This will really help me to be more responsible."

I don't think so. I don't think the boy was doing any quiet reflecting. I suspect that he was mostly experiencing emotions, such as fear, anger, humiliation, and hurt. If my discernment is correct, the boy was submissive on the outside but hurt and angry on the inside.

When the father had finished his harangue, he paused, still panting from the angry lecture. Then he bellowed: "I love you." He set his son down and returned to pick up the conversation with me.

---

72 This story adapted from *The Frightful and Joyous Journey of Family Life* by the author.

Again, let's take the child's perspective. Do you think the boy felt loved? Do you think he felt safe and cherished? I don't think so. I think he was hurt. The person who should be his friend, protector, teacher, and advocate had acted with disregard for him and his feelings. The father had expressed his own anger. Even though he loved his son very much, he had not acted in his son's best interest. He had not sent a clear message.

Let's re-write the bike-parking script with love and learning as the themes. When Dad spotted the bike parked in a forbidden place, Dad might have called out to his son, "Come here, Son! Let's talk." Dad could kneel by his boy and ask, "Did you notice where you parked your bike?" It seems likely that the boy would immediately remember the rule. Dad could show compassion. "It's hard to remember when you're in a hurry. What could we do to help you remember?" The son might suggest, "Dad, could we take some chalk and draw a parking place for my bike on the floor?" Because the son was a vital part of the solution, he is much more likely to remember it.

With this approach, the parent sends a clear message: "I love you, Son. And I want to help you grow toward peaceful, loving, safe, adulthood."

Reflection:

Think of a time when you have sent a clear message to one of your children when you were tempted to send a mixed or angry message.
How did it feel? _____

_____

_____

What helped you get there? _____

_____

_____

How can you get there again? _____

_____

_____

How can you make that experience more common for you?_____

_____

_____

Applying this strategy:

☐ I ask Father for help.

☐ I remember (with gratitude) past successes with this strategy.

☐ I ask myself, does this strategy fit me? If not, can I adapt it or should I discard it?

☐ I plan my response for next time the challenge arises.

☐ I imagine or pre-experience the better way of responding.

☐ I try it out.

☐ I keep refining my efforts—otherwise known as repenting.

Notes on my progress: _____

_____

_____

_____

_____

_____

52. Get the help of ancestors.

There are people who have even more knowledge and perhaps greater skills for helping our families than we do: Our ancestors. Consider the words of President Faust at the April 2006 General Conference:

> In ancient and modern times angels have appeared and given instruction, warnings, and direction, which benefited the people they visited. We do not consciously realize the extent to which ministering angels affect our lives. President Joseph F. Smith said, "In like manner *our fathers and mothers, brothers, sisters and friends who have passed away from this earth, having been faithful, and worthy to enjoy these rights and privileges, may have a mission given them to visit their relatives and friends upon the earth again, bringing from the divine Presence messages of love, of warning, or reproof and instruction, to those whom they had learned to love in the flesh.*" Many of us feel that we have had this experience. Their ministry has been and is an important part of the gospel.[73]

I am one of those who feels that he has had that experience. At a time when I felt confused and anxious about decisions that Nancy and I needed to make, I didn't know where to turn for help. In desperation I found a room alone and asked counsel from my dear and wise father who had died a few months earlier. Though my ears did not hear a thing, his counsel and comfort came to me as clearly as if he had been sitting in the room with me.

Citing a story told by President David O. McKay, President Benson encouraged us to be open to impressions:

> A son of Bishop and Sister Wells was killed in a railroad accident in Salt Lake canyon. He was run over by a freight train. Sister

---

73 James E. Faust, "A Royal Priesthood," *Ensign*, May 2006, 51, emphasis added.

Wells could not be comforted at the loss. She felt no relief from her sorrow during the funeral and continued her mourning after her son's burial. Bishop Wells was concerned for her health, as she was in a state of deep anguish.

One day, soon after the funeral, Sister Wells was lying on her bed in a state of mourning. The son appeared to her and said, "Mother, do not mourn, do not cry. I am all right."

He then told her how the accident took place. Apparently there had been some question about how the accident had happened because the young man was an experienced railroad man. But he told his mother that it was clearly an accident.

Now note this: He also told her that as soon as he realized that he was beyond the mortal world, he had tried to reach his father but could not. His father was so busy with the details of his work that he could not respond to the promptings of the Spirit. Therefore, the son had come to his mother.

He then said, "Tell Father that all is well with me, and I want you not to mourn any more."[74]

How many times might we get needed reassurance and counsel from our ancestors if we sought it? I'm not sure just how we access the help of ancestors. I suppose that we call on them when we have special needs. Or we just open ourselves to them. And we listen. President Benson drew from the story above that we should take time to meditate. When we do, our family members who have past on may give us specific impressions. They may open the way before us. They may comfort our souls.

It would be a shame to fail to use the wealth of loving and capable family members who are on the other side of the veil. As Elisha taught his helper:

---

74 Ezra Taft Benson, "Seek the Spirit of the Lord," *Tambali*, Sept. 1988, 2.

"Fear not: for they that be with us are more than they that be with them" (2 Kings 6:16). Elisha opened his servant's eyes to see that the mountains were filled with willing helpers.

Reflection:

Think of a time when you have gotten help from your ancestors—or think of ways you could get their help.

How did it—or could it—feel? _____

_____

_____

What helped you get there? _____

_____

_____

How can you get there again? _____

_____

How can you make that experience more common for you?_____

_____

_____

Applying this strategy:

☐ I ask Father for help.

☐ I remember (with gratitude) past successes with this strategy.

☐ I ask myself, does this strategy fit me? If not, can I adapt it or should I discard it?

☐ I plan my response for next time the challenge arises.

☐ I imagine or pre-experience the better way of responding.

☐ I try it out.

☐ I keep refining my efforts—otherwise known as repenting.

Notes on my progress: _____

_____

_____

_____

_____

_____

_____

53. Imitate Jesus. 📖

I am not proud of the fact that I often played a stalling game with my son Andy. When he was a little boy he would ask me to take a walk around the block with him. I would tell him that I would be glad to go—as soon as I finished reading the paper. Andy saw through my ruse: "That's what you always say, Dad."

I had been caught. So I jumped up and said, "Let's go." I dashed out the front door and headed around the block. As I rounded the first corner, Andy was still back in the front yard inspecting stones and bugs. I yelled, "Come on, Andy! We've got to get around the block!"

I wanted to be a good dad. I loved my son. But I was stingy with my time. For all of us mortals who regularly lose our perspective on eternity, Jesus is the perfect example.

> And they brought young children to him, that he should touch them: and his disciples rebuked those that brought them.
>
> But when Jesus saw it, he was much displeased, and said unto them, Suffer the little children to come unto me, and forbid them not: for of such is the kingdom of God.
>
> Verily I say unto you, Whosoever shall not receive the kingdom of God as a little child, he shall not enter therein.
>
> And he took them up in his arms, put his hands upon them, and blessed them. (Mark 10:13–16)

Often we turn children away as an interruption or an intrusion. Jesus was different. He knew that nothing in the world was more important than being with children. "He took them up in his arms, put his hands upon them, and blessed them." Wow. Those children knew they were loved. They had the undivided attention of the Great Appreciator.

Elder Melvin J. Ballard told what it is like to be in the arms of Jesus:

> I found myself one evening in the dreams of the night in that sacred building, the temple. After a season of prayer and rejoicing I was informed that I should have the privilege of entering into one of those rooms, to meet a glorious Personage, and, as I entered the door, I saw, seated on a raised platform, the most glorious Being my eyes have ever beheld or that I ever conceived existed in all the eternal worlds. As I approached to be introduced, he arose and stepped towards me with extended arms, and he smiled as he softly spoke my name. If I shall live to be a million years old, I shall never forget that smile. He took me into his arms and kissed me, pressed me to his bosom, and blessed me, until the marrow of my bones seemed to melt! When he had finished, I knelt at his feet, and, as I bathed them with my tears and kisses, I saw the prints of the nails in the feet of the Redeemer of the world. The feeling that I had in the presence of him who hath all things in his hands, to have his love, his affection, and his blessing was such that if I ever can receive that of which I had but a foretaste, I would give all that I am, all that I ever hope to be, to feel what I then felt.[75]

It can be our goal to offer that same kind of graciousness and love to our children. They come to seek the Divine as they see it in us.

---

75 Bryant S. Hinckley, *Sermons and Missionary Service of Melvin J. Ballard* (Salt Lake City: Deseret Book, 1949), 155–56.

I'm quite sure that we can never represent Jesus well enough—unless we let him take up occupancy in our souls. When he fills us up, hardness, resentment, and anger disappear. They are swallowed up by goodness.

Getting Christ fully settled in our souls is the work of a lifetime. We tend to throw him out when we need him most. We must turn ourselves over to him. The desires of our heart must be to pray as Fenelon prayed:

> Lord, I know not what I ought to ask of thee; Thou only knowest what I need; Thou lovest me better than I know how to love myself. O Father! give to Thy child that which he himself knows not how to ask. I dare not ask either for crosses or consolations: I simply present myself before Thee, I open my heart to Thee. Behold my needs which I know not myself; see and do according to Thy tender mercy. Smite, or heal; depress me, or raise me up: I adore all thy purposes without knowing them; I am silent; I offer myself in sacrifice; I yield myself to Thee; I would have no other desire than to accomplish Thy will. Teach me to pray. Pray Thyself in me. Amen.[76]

President Benson reminded us, "Finally, men captained by Christ will be consumed in Christ. To paraphrase President Harold B. Lee, they set fire in others because they are on fire. Their will is swallowed up in his will. They do always those things that please the Lord. Not only would they die for the Lord, but more important, they want to live for him."[77]

We become soft-spoken parents as he speaks through us. When Andy—or one of his children—wants to take a walk around the block, I hope I will always be available. I hope I will drop the paper and take his hand and let him lead me toward Heaven.

---

76 Francois de la Mothe Fenelon quoted in Harry Emerson Fosdick, *Meaning of Prayer* (New York: Association Press, 1915), 58–59.

77 *The Teachings of Ezra Taft Benson* (Salt Lake City: Bookcraft, 1988), 329.

Reflection:

Think of a time when you have imitated Christ.

How did it feel? _____

_____

_____

What helped you get there? _____

_____

_____

How can you get there again? _____

_____

_____

How can you make that experience more common for you?_____

_____

_____

Applying this strategy:

☐ I ask Father for help.

☐ I remember (with gratitude) past successes with this strategy.

☐ I ask myself, does this strategy fit me? If not, can I adapt it or should I discard it?

☐ I plan my response for next time the challenge arises.

☐ I imagine or pre-experience the better way of responding.

☐ I try it out.

☐ I keep refining my efforts—otherwise known as repenting.

Notes on my progress: _____

_____

_____

_____

_____

54. Rewrite the story.

A mother caught me after a parenting workshop seeking advice. She began, "Last night while my daughter was studying, I cooked dinner for her. It's something she loves. When I took it to her, she turned up her nose at it. I was indignant. I chewed her out and told her she was grounded for a week for acting that way." Mom paused before proceeding, "The punishment seems extreme. But I don't want to go back on my word. What should I do?" Both mom and daughter felt awful about the confrontation. And both were trapped in their remoteness.

The mother wisely recognized that making threats and failing to enforce them sends mixed messages to children. Yet, as parents, we don't need to be trapped by past mistakes. There is another option. I recommended that they rewrite the story:

"This afternoon when your daughter gets home from school, ask her if you can take some time to visit. When you are comfortably seated, tell her that you were upset last night. You felt that your daughter was not very appreciative. Then, in the spirit of repentance, you can acknowledge that your reaction was not one you feel good about. You took her lack of appreciation personally and reacted emotionally. Ask her if you could both erase last night and start over again. Tell her that you love her more than life itself and you never want a small misunderstanding to become a big barrier between you."

The mother looked very relieved by the suggestion. She knew what would happen after the new beginning to the old story. She knew that her daughter would grab her mother and apologize. She knew that they would once again be joined in love. Grounding was superfluous.

Some time in the future the daughter will again be unappreciative. It is inevitable. But Mom has scripted a better reaction. She might say, "Ouch! I had hoped to delight you with one of your favorite meals. I'm disappointed that you're not pleased." When the daughter knows her mother's intentions, she is likely to react more gently. It is also possible that Mom would ask the daughter if she would like her to make a snack for her before investing the effort.

Repentance is nothing more than the continuing process of learning to be wiser and better under the tutoring and grace of God.

Reflection:

Think of a time when you have rewritten a sad story—when you have gone back to repair an unhelpful reaction.

How did it feel? _____

_____

_____

What helped you get there? _____

_____

_____

How can you get there again? _____

_____

How can you make that experience more common for you?_____

_____

_____

Applying this strategy:

☐ I ask Father for help.

☐ I remember (with gratitude) past successes with this strategy.

☐ I ask myself, does this strategy fit me? If not, can I adapt it or should I discard it?

☐ I plan my response for next time the challenge arises.

☐ I imagine or pre-experience the better way of responding.

☐ I try it out.

☐ I keep refining my efforts—otherwise known as repenting.

Notes on my progress: _____

_____

_____

_____

_____

_____

_____

55. Get God's help.

None of this is easy. None of it is natural—since the natural parent is an enemy to God and to his children. But it is possible. We can "become a saint through the atonement of Christ the Lord" (Mosiah 3:19). When we have faith unto repentance—what a great phrase!—miracles are possible. Faith unto repentance—enough trust in God to turn our lives over to him.

President Hinckley taught us beautifully when he told the following story:

> Included in that panel was an attractive and able young woman, divorced, the mother of seven children then ranging in ages from five to sixteen. She said that one evening she went across the street to deliver something to a neighbor. Listen to her words as I recall them:

> "As I turned around to walk back home, I could see my house lighted up. I could hear echoes of my children as I had walked out of the door a few minutes earlier: 'Mom, what are we going to have for dinner?' 'Can you take me to the library?' 'I have to get some poster paper tonight.' Tired and weary, I looked at that house and saw the light on in each of the rooms. I thought of all of those children who were home waiting for me to come and meet their needs. My burdens felt very heavy on my shoulders.

> "I remember looking through tears toward the sky, and I said, 'Oh, my Father, I just can't do it tonight. I'm too tired. I can't face it. I can't go home and take care of all those children alone. Could I just come to You and stay with You for just one night? I'll come back in the morning.'

"I didn't really hear the words of reply, but I heard them in my mind. The answer was, 'No, little one, you can't come to me now. You would never wish to come back. But I can come to you.'"[78]

He can come to us. And when he does, everything changes.

Reflection:

Think of a time when you have drawn God into your life.
How did it feel? _____
_____
_____

What helped you get there? _____
_____
_____

How can you get there again? _____
_____
_____

How can you make that experience more common for you? _____
_____
_____

Applying this strategy:

☐ I ask Father for help.
☐ I remember (with gratitude) past successes with this strategy.
☐ I ask myself, does this strategy fit me? If not, can I adapt it or should I discard it?

---

78 Gordon B. Hinckley, "What God Hath Joined Together," *Ensign*, May 1991, 73.

☐ I plan my response for next time the challenge arises.

☐ I imagine or pre-experience the better way of responding.

☐ I try it out.

☐ I keep refining my efforts—otherwise known as repenting.

Notes on my progress: _____

_____

_____

_____

_____

_____

_____

Conclusion

I hope this book has been useful to you. I hope it has given specific ideas and general encouragement. It may also have given some pain.

Yet I believe that pain is our friend. Just as the person with a numb foot runs the risk of injuring the foot unawares, so the person who is unaware of shortcomings runs the risk of harming his or her spirit unawares.

Mercifully, heaven discloses our shortcomings to us in manageable doses:

> And if men come unto me I will show unto them their weakness. I give unto men weakness that they may be humble; and my grace is sufficient for all men that humble themselves before me; for if they humble themselves before me, and have faith in me, then will I make weak things become strong unto them. (Ether 12:27)

As you have read the various prescriptions in this book, you may have become aware of painful shortcomings. But if we humble ourselves before God, and have faith in him, he will make those weaknesses become strengths.

How do we know if we are doing as much as the Lord expects of us as parents? I have often felt: "Some parents seem to do so well while I fumble along, making so many mistakes! What is wrong with me?" I take comfort in the Lord's startling definition of righteousness found in Luke. His instruction and some parenthetic comments follow.

> And he spake this parable unto certain which trusted in themselves that they were righteous [parents], and despised others:

Two men went up into the temple to pray; the one a Pharisee, and the other a publican.

The Pharisee stood and prayed thus with himself, God, I thank thee, that I am not as other men are, extortioners, unjust, adulterers, or even as this publican. [And I am thankful that *my* children are not on drugs or in trouble with the law.]

I fast twice in the week, I give tithes of all that I possess. [We hold regular family home evening, and family prayer...]

And the publican, standing afar off, would not lift up so much as his eyes unto heaven, but smote upon his breast, saying, God be merciful to me a sinner. [I make so many mistakes! I lose my temper, I fail to understand my children, I neglect prayer...]

I tell you, this man went down to his house justified rather than the other: for every one that exalteth himself shall be abased; and he that humbleth himself shall be [Note this key word for Latter-day Saints:] exalted[!] (Luke 18:9–14).

It is not the parent who seems to do it all perfectly who will be exalted. It is the one who recognizes his own failings and calls upon Father with all the energy of his heart. Parenting classes may give us good ideas for dealing with children. Talking with wise and tender friends may help us. But, if we are to excel at parenting, we must have divine help.

It should be no surprise that some of the greatest trials of our lives come in parenting and family life. Only a task that demands the sacrifice of all our pride, all our self-importance, and all our stubbornness has the power to make us perfect.[79] Our family challenges on earth prepare us for a fullness of family joy in which we will enjoy not only our earthly family but also throngs of loved ones whom we may not have seen since our earth lives began. At that great day every knee will bow and every tongue will confess... not because his power commands it, but because we are mystified and humbled by his inexpressible goodness and wisdom.

It is a good beginning to know his remarkable goodness, but it is not enough. Joseph Smith reported the following vision:

> I saw the Twelve Apostles of the Lamb, who are now upon the earth, who hold the keys of this last ministry, in foreign lands, standing together in a circle, much fatigued, with their clothes tattered and feet swollen, with their eyes cast downward, and Jesus standing in their midst, and they did not behold him. The Savior looked upon them and wept.[80]

Very often in our parenting experience we may be weary and downcast. We may not know that the Savior is in our midst, ready to help us.

Our desperation in parenting is very useful if it leads us to call upon Jesus in total humility. We may remember the greatness of God, and our own nothingness, and humble ourselves, calling on the name of the Lord daily (see Mosiah 4:11). We may call out, "Father, I'm trying so hard and doing so imperfectly! Please, help me! Please pour out thy perfect grace on my weak soul!" There is a surprising peace that settles in on us when we stop trying to be super-parents and recognize our dependence upon God.

Adult faith, the kind necessary for effective parenting, goes beyond acknowledging that he exists. It celebrates his remarkable ability to turn

---

79 See Joseph Smith's *Lectures on Faith*, Lecture 6, Number 7.
80 Joseph Smith, *History of the Church* 2:381.

everything to our good and to provide us with every lesson necessary for exaltation. We call upon Father and trust serenely knowing that he will provide the experiences that will bless and perfect us.

We draw on his power when we gladly repent. No parent gets it right the first time. We all make lots of mistakes. Consider the wise counsel from Moroni: "yea, teach parents that they must repent and be baptized, and humble themselves as their little children, and they shall all be saved with their little children" (Moroni 8:10).

But repentance is more than making the same mistake over and over again and feeling bad about it. Father expects us to keep looking for better ways. We observe and seek counsel from those who seem to exemplify the teachings of Jesus. We yearn to find better ways. And we study Jesus' life for the perfect example. Repentance is learning.

So, does the atonement of Jesus Christ have anything to do with our effectiveness as parents? Yes. It allows us to be born into this world innocent. It provides the power for us to come to Christ in faith and to be filled with that perfect love that we call charity. It provides the power for us to be changed, cleansed, refreshed, renewed, and filled with the divine nature. It provides the power to rescue us from our sins of attitude and action. And Jesus' life of love and service provides the perfect example for us to study. Jesus and his atonement provide the only hope for us as parents. He can truly make us at one with him and with beloved family members.

Perhaps my all-time favorite parenting story is of a kindergartner named Terry who showed up at school one day with a note pinned to his jacket. He displayed the note proudly to his classmates. Eventually the teacher spotted the note. Wondering if it had important instructions for her, she asked Terry, "Would you like me to read your note?" "Yes, I would." The teacher removed the note and read: "Terry was unhappy this morning because his sister had a note and he did not. So this is Terry's note, and now he is happy." That is grace.

May we respond to Elder Maxwell's invitation: "Let us make our way, righteously and resolutely, notwithstanding our weaknesses, to the beckoning City of God. There the sole and self-assigned gatekeeper is Jesus Christ. He awaits us at the gate not only to *certify* us—but because his deep, divine desire brings him there to *welcome* us. 'He employeth no servant there' (2 Nephi 9:41). If we acknowledge him now, he will lovingly acknowledge us then."[81]

Jesus has taught us why we should listen to his counsel: "Listen to him who is the advocate [Advocate! Not accuser, but advocate!] with the Father, who is pleading your cause [Pleading my cause? Thanks be to heaven!] before him" (D&C 45:3).

We might half expect that he will take us to the Father and apologetically present us: "Father, here is [Fill in your name.] He was a pretty good guy. Yeah, I know. He made a lot of mistakes.... In fact, he made some really stupid mistakes. But he tried hard and he did a few good things."

In our telestial way of thinking, we almost imagine that Jesus will weakly plead our cause and then step out of the way to see if we can cut some kind of deal with a Father who has every reason to be disappointed with us. But that is *not* what he does. Jesus describes his pleading for us: "Father, behold the sufferings and death of him who did no sin, in whom thou wast well pleased; behold the blood of thy Son which was shed, the blood of him whom thou gavest that thyself might be glorified" (D&C 45:4).

---

81 Neal A. Maxwell, "True Believers in Christ," *Speeches*, 7 October 1980, Brigham Young University, http://speeches. byu.edu/reader/reader.php?id=6769

Being mortals we rather expect him to follow this grand presentation of himself by suggesting that he be given the best seat in the Heavenly House and that maybe some of his buddies be admitted. Once again he surprises us. After presenting the inexpressible merits of his goodness, he steps behind us and pushes us to Father: "Wherefore, Father, spare these my brethren that believe on my name, that they may come unto me and have everlasting life" (D&C 45:5).

Hold everything! After presenting the merits of his remarkable goodness, he applies that goodness to us so that we can join him and Father in the Heavenly Home? He lived, taught, suffered, and died only so that he could rescue us? We have reason to ask as did Ammon, "*Who could have supposed* that our God would have been so merciful as to have snatched us from our awful, sinful, and polluted state?" (Alma 26:17, emphasis added). He who is truly First pushes each believer ahead of him in line and becomes the Last.

Oh, how we ought to thank our Heavenly King![82] He has given us the opportunity to learn from our mortal experiences and to be ultimately rescued from our mistakes by his goodness.

---

82 See Mosiah 2:19.

About the Author

Wally Goddard, PH.D. is unique in the
way he combines scholarship, faith in
the Gospel of Jesus Christ, and sheer joy.
He got his PhD in Family and Human
Development and is currently a professor
of Family Life for the University of
Arkansas Cooperative Extension where
he develops programs on well-being, marriage, and parenting. He has written
books for LDS, general, and professional audiences and served on national
committees on parenting and marriage. He has served in the church as a
bishop, high councilor, and institute teacher. He describes his wife, Nancy,
as most soft-spoken and charitable parent he knows. Wally and Nancy have
three adult children and a growing number of amazing grandchildren..

What His Family Says:
"His presentations and books are filled with optimism, enthusiasm, and
charity; just what he is! He loves people, especially his family. His wife,
children and grandchildren will testify that he is the most loving, perceptive,
and creative husband, dad, and grandpa ever. He is a joy to be around and his
greatest desire is to help others."   —Nancy (wife)

"Wally Goddard (aka, Bapa) switched careers mid-life from being a math and
science teacher to his true calling in Family and Human Development. His
grandkids think he's a blast, but still has a lot to learn. Buy this book anyway."
 —Emily (daughter)

"Dad's life is a quest for greater knowledge, but not just any knowledge. He
reaches for the highest possible good - Family Joy!"—Andy (son)

Gabe may be only a little boy, but he says you should read this book immediately.
                    —Sara (daughter)